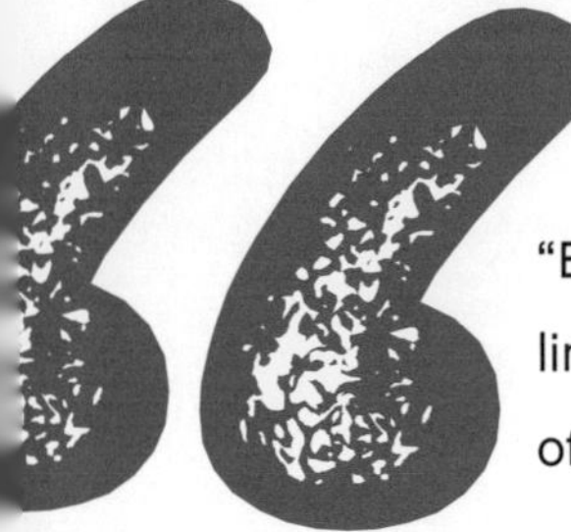

"Bonnie Neubauer's *The Write-Brain Workbook* is chock-a-block with exercises to limber a writer's imagination and shake loose dust bunnies from the brain, while offering up sound advice and encouragement. Hard work isn't usually this much fun."

—HALLIE EPHRON, *NEW YORK TIMES* BEST-SELLING AUTHOR OF *NIGHT NIGHT, SLEEP TIGHT* AND THE EDGAR-NOMINATED *WRITING AND SELLING YOUR MYSTERY NOVEL*

"*The Write-Brain Workbook* is a treasure trove of writerly gems—from ridiculously fun exercises for character building and story creation to madcap methods for conquering writer's block. If you're stuck, if you're embarking on a new project, or if you just need a jolt of creative lightning, this book will provide it!"

—SHEREE BYKOFSKY, LITERARY AGENT AND FOUNDER OF SHEREE BYKOFSKY ASSOCIATES, INC.

"Writers who struggle with daily practice or making time to write will find *The Write-Brain Workbook* a joyful solution. It offers irresistible, fun challenges to spark creativity and story ideas, every day of the year."

—JANE FRIEDMAN, AUTHOR AND PROFESSOR

"Bonnie Neubauer's *The Write-Brain Workbook* is bursting at the seams with vividly illustrated, creativity-inducing explorations and exercises. Each stand-alone activity is an unforgettable adventure and writing experience with just the right amount of humor."

—CHRIS DUNMIRE, CREATIVITY COACH AND FOUNDER OF THE AWARD-WINNING CREATIVITY PORTAL (WWW.CREATIVITY-PORTAL.COM)

"This is the most irresistible book I've read in a long time. Whether you use it to break out of a block, strengthen your writing muscles, or just have fun, it's guaranteed to spark your creativity and bring joy back to your writing process. A perfect gift for writer-friends, too!"

—JENNA GLATZER,
BEST-SELLING AUTHOR AND GHOSTWRITER

"Normally I don't get excited about 'writing exercises'—possibly because they all start to look the same. That was, until I looked at Bonnie Neubauer's book and thought, *Hey, these look like FUN!* It's impossible to flip through the pages of this book without getting drawn in—and once you get hooked, you'll want to keep going. This book is perfect for anyone who needs to jumpstart—or restart—their writing spark."

—MOIRA ALLEN, EDITOR OF WRITING-WORLD.COM AND
AUTHOR OF *STARTING YOUR CAREER AS A FREELANCE WRITER*

"If you have trouble getting started with writing a chapter or a book, then you need to get *The Write-Brain Workbook*. The exercises in this book will get your creative fires burning and knock your writer's block off its block."

—JOHN KREMER, AUTHOR OF
1001 WAYS TO MARKET YOUR BOOKS

"Ever have trouble getting started writing? No more. Just pick up a copy of *The Write-Brain Workbook* and free the writer within you. These creative, out-of-the-box daily exercises will help you start fast and keep on writing."

—BUD GARDNER, CO-AUTHOR OF
CHICKEN SOUP FOR THE WRITER'S SOUL

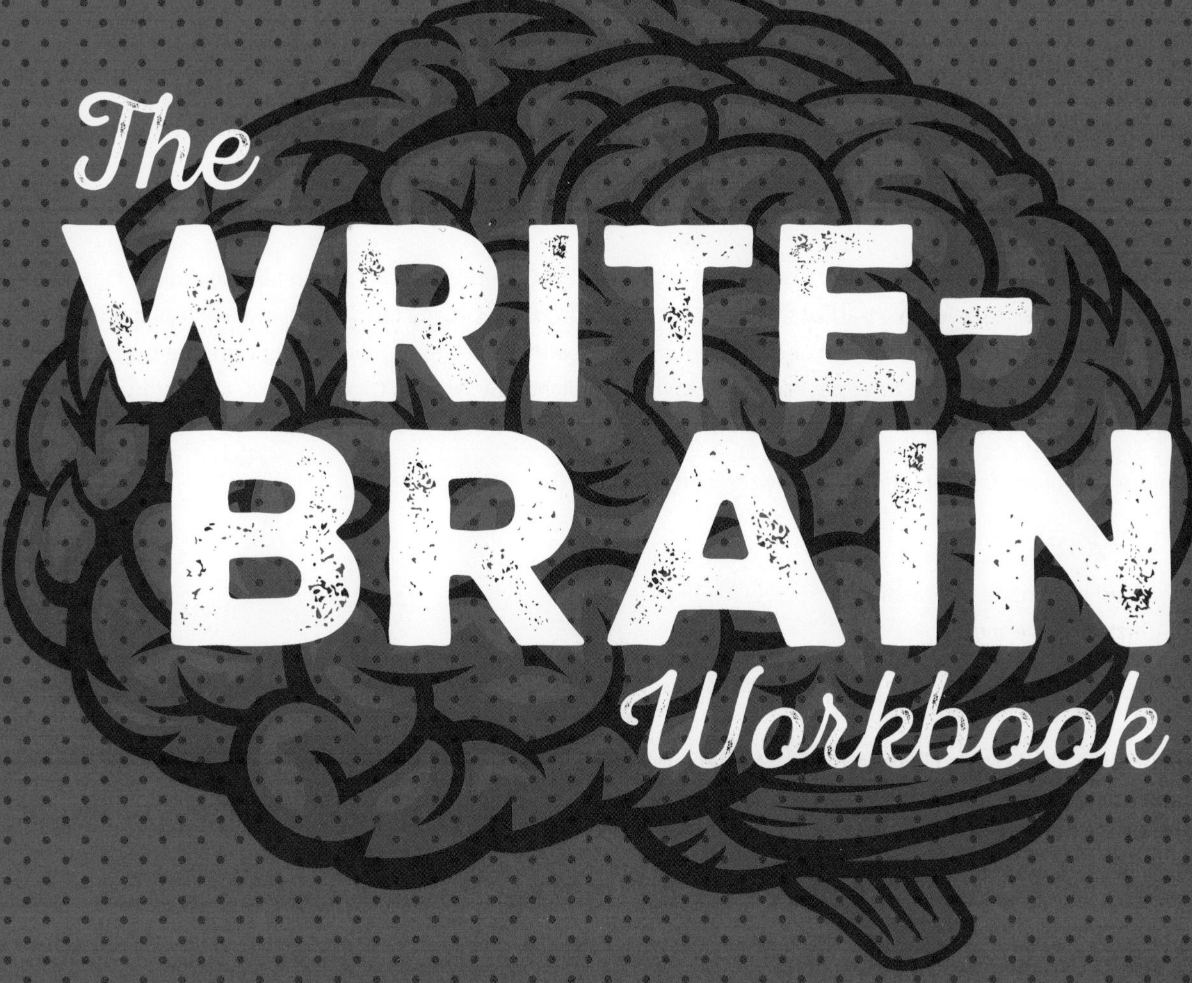

The WRITE-BRAIN Workbook

REVISED & EXPANDED

BONNIE **NEUBAUER**

WRITER'S DIGEST BOOKS

WritersDigest.com
Cincinnati, Ohio

 Published by Writer's Digest Books, an imprint of F+W Media, Inc., 10151 Carver Road, Suite # 200, Blue Ash, OH 45242. (800)289-0963. Revised edition.

For more resources for writers, visit www.writersdigest.com.

19 18 17 16 5 4 3

Distributed in Canada by Fraser Direct
100 Armstrong Avenue
Georgetown, Ontario, Canada L7G 5S4
Tel: (905) 877-4411

Distributed in the U.K. and Europe by F&W Media International
Brunel House, Newton Abbot, Devon, TQ12 4PU, England
Tel: (+44) 1626-323200, Fax: (+44) 1626-323319
E-mail: postmaster@davidandcharles.co.uk

Distributed in Australia by Capricorn Link
P.O. Box 704, Windsor, NSW 2756 Australia
Tel: (02) 4577-3555

ISBN-13: 978-1-59963-838-6

EDITED BY Rachel Randall
DESIGNED BY Alexis Brown and Claudean Wheeler
PRODUCTION COORDINATED BY Debbie Thomas

ABOUT THE AUTHOR

Photo credit: Jayne Toohey

Bonnie Neubauer is the author of motivational writing books: *The Write-Brain Workbook Revised & Expanded* (Writer's Digest Books), *303 Writing Prompts: Ideas to Get You Started* (Fall River Press/Sterling Publishing), and *Take Ten for Writers* (Writer's Digest Books). She is also the inventor of Story Spinner, a handheld and digital tool for generating millions of creative writing exercises.

When she's not dreaming up writing prompts or running fun and funny workshops, Bonnie can be found playing, teaching, or designing board games. With her love of words and language, it's no surprise her first published game, ADJitation (BreakingGames.com), contains sixty-four cubes with different adjectives on all sides.

Bonnie lives in suburban Philadelphia surrounded by more than a few of her favorite things, including her books, games, iPad, cats, extended family, and wonderful husband. Follow her on Twitter @NeuBon, or check out her (rarely updated) website, www.BonnieNeubauer.com.

DEDICATION

To my love, Gil—forever and a day.

ACKNOWLEDGMENTS

Had I not insisted we squeeze 400 exercises into fewer than 400 pages, I'd have more room to thank everyone individually. Alas, in this tiny paragraph, I offer a huge group hug of thanks to family, friends, employers, book buyers and sellers, aspiring writers, workshop attendees, my students, all meeples, and everyone in my life who supports and encourages—or at least tolerates—my never-ending creativity habit.

Rachel Randall, the entire team at Writer's Digest Books and F+W Media, and Jennifer DeChiara: You all rock! Here's to at least another ten years.

FOREWORD

Writers often try to think and reason their way through material that's tricky or sticky. Surely the answer to the perfect scene, captivating dialogue, or great character development is hiding somewhere in your mind, if only you could concentrate hard enough. Unfortunately, when we're stuck somewhere in our writing, our usual methods are often inroads to frustration.

Thankfully, *The Write Brain Workbook Revised and Expanded* is the perfect antidote to writer's block—that feeling of being stuck or bored with your writing. This workbook offers a world of whimsy with 400 unique and inquisitive exercises. When I began working through the exercises, I was stalled, as I often am, in the middle of writing my novel. When I get stuck, I also have the unpleasant tendency of projecting negative qualities onto all aspects of my writing skills: *I can't write a novel because I'm no good; I'm lazy; my idea is undeveloped.* But once I allowed myself the pleasure of play, my writing engine was running again.

The Write-Brain Workbook is the opposite of work. By exploring the astonishing breadth of exercises, which play upon the senses as well as the intellect, you may, as I did, find yourself laughing. Feeling light. Playing like a little kid. Bonnie Neubauer's exercises wake up the magic of writing that sometimes gets lost in the day-to-day work.

Many of us fall back on routines and habits that we take for granted because we just don't know any other way. But this book helps you shake free of constrictive methods in favor of utterly fresh ones. Every page encourages you to take a different approach to writing. Whether you're penning a story inside different shapes (no, really), trying out wild new similes, or using petite snippets of your own memory to generate stories, Neubauer offers you prompts you probably wouldn't think of on your own. Every page is a mind tickler.

With clever puns ("vocal-eyes" instead of *vocalize*; an exercise in which you describe a character by how he or she sounds) and wild whimsy that appeals to the parts of your brain that aren't normally in charge during a writing session, you'll come away refreshed, challenged (but only in fun ways), and excited about writing again. Writers often give too much power to the idea of inspiration—as though it only strikes with a force as rare and powerful as lightning. These exercises will banish this notion and wake up surprising stores of material you hadn't realized were there all along, waiting to be excavated.

What's more, the book plays beautifully off its inventive visuals: startling colors, geometric shapes, and surprising juxtapositions of poetry and composition that stimulate both sides of your brain.

This book wonderfully reminds us that sometimes the most serious way to tackle our writing is not to take ourselves too seriously. Rather, we need to tease creativity out of hiding through silly adventures down side alleys and unfamiliar paths.

I dare any writer to attempt even a week's worth of exercises in *The Write-Brain Workbook* and then continue to write the same way. I don't think it's possible.

What are you waiting for? Dive in.

Jordan Rosenfeld

JORDAN E. ROSENFELD is the author of three novels, most recently *Woman in Red*, and four writing guides, including *Writing Deep Scenes*, with Martha Alderson; *A Writer's Guide to Persistence*; *Make a Scene*; and *Write Free*, with Rebecca Lawton. Her essays and articles have appeared in such publications as *Alternet*, *Bustle*, *Creative Live*, *Family Fun*, Mom.me, *The New York Times*, *The Rumpus*, *Salon*, *San Francisco Chronicle*, *The Washington Post*, *The Weeklings*, *Writer's Digest*, and many more. Her book commentaries have appeared on *The California Report*, produced by NPR affiliate KQED radio. She created and hosted the literary radio program "Word by Word: Conversations with Writers" on KRCB, which won an NEA Chairman's grant in 2004. She and Martha Alderson co-lead Writer Path retreats: www.writerpath.com. Visit her website: www.jordanrosenfeld.net.

INTRODUCTION

Hi. My name is Bonnie Neubauer, and I am thrilled to welcome you to *The Write-Brain Workbook Revised and Expanded.* This book is unlike other creative writing books in that you will *not spend your time reading about writing.* Instead, you will jump right in and immediately write—right in the book. All you need is a pen and about ten spare minutes to enjoy this at-home workshop in a workbook format.

All the exercises are designed to get you writing and keep you writing, because the more you write, the better you write. While having a blast with the exercises, you will be able to watch yourself improve. You have my promise that along the way you will never face the dreaded blank page—every exercise gives you something to build from: a starting phrase, an ending sentence, a series of challenging words to incorporate, a fill-in-the-blanks character to create ... and so much more.

When you flip through the book, you will notice the colorful and visually engaging art on every page. Full credit for this brilliance goes to the amazing design team at Writer's Digest Books. I owe them a huge thank-you because, when it comes to art, I struggle with stick figures.

If you're wondering whom this book is for, well, it's perfect for anyone age nine and older who would like to try their hand at writing. It's not just for novices, however. Experienced writers looking to experiment with creative writing will find it very beneficial and eye opening. And if you happen to be experiencing writer's block, the exercises within these covers are the ideal antidote, as they remove preconceived expectations by prompting you to write about unexpected topics. The exercises are also fantastic warm-ups before you settle into your "real" writing. If you keep a journal, you'll feel right at home since many of the exercises use personal experience as a jumping block. If you are a creative writing workshop junkie, you'll no longer have to wait until the next workshop. You can do these exercises alone, at home, or on vacation, or you can even create your own writing group and do them with your friends. With a little editing and polishing, you can likely turn many of the results of these exercises into stories, poems, articles, or even novels to be submitted for publication.

On each page you will find a bonus exercise titled **TAKE THE NEXT STEP.** These will help you learn about your writing practice preferences and assist you as you explore your personal writing process. These simple lessons can be applied immediately to your other writing, too.

On some pages you will see the icon to the left. It denotes exercises that can be done multiple times with unique setups. Make sure you mark these pages so you remember to return to them.

One more thing before I unleash you to write: I was a tad overzealous when creating content for this book, so Writer's Digest had to leave some exercises on the cutting room floor. When they saw how chagrined I was about that, they generously offered to create an online page of bonus exercises, available to all who purchase the book. The access link is www.writersdigest.com/write-brain-workbook-revised.

On page viii you will find some basic rules and guidelines to follow when doing the writing exercises in this book. If you don't happen to like following rules (which makes you a bit like me), then the rules are there for you to rebel against. Either way, it's time to dive in and start writing.

I wish you much joy as you play with your words and go on the multitude of writing adventures that await you in this book. **WRITE ON!**

Bonnie

A special thank-you to the hundreds upon hundreds of writers who have attended my workshops, and the thousands upon thousands of writers and teachers who have bought my writing books and Story Spinner. Your enthusiasm for writing and dedication to the craft is both humbling and contagious.

THE RULES

Here are some basic rules and guidelines to follow when doing the writing exercises in this book.

- **KEEP WRITING:** This is the number-one way to maintain your momentum. Don't stop; keep writing and moving forward. If you hit a block and don't know what to write next, write the last word over and over until something new starts flowing. Usually it's the word *and*. Write "and, and, and, and, and, and," and soon you will be writing, "I am sick of writing the word *and*. I am also sick of ..." And you're off and writing again.

- **DON'T EDIT:** Editing is left-brain work that stops your momentum in its tracks—and these exercises are designed for right-brain fun. Don't go back and cross out or change words. If you can't think of a particular word, draw a blank line and keep writing. At the end of the writing session, the line will remind you that you wanted to search for a word. Don't worry about spelling or grammar (with apologies to all the English teachers out there); there's plenty of time for that later. Just make sure you can read what you write.

- **LET YOURSELF GO:** Don't worry about the end result. Give yourself permission to throw words on the page. Don't hold back or filter yourself. You don't have to show it to anyone, so go on an adventure and play with your ideas and words.

- **BE SPECIFIC:** Use all your senses to describe things. Use your sense of smell to describe a computer, your sense of taste to describe a taxicab. The best way for a reader to recall what you've written is to be specific: not "toy," but "plastic Batman figure missing an arm." If you find that when you focus on being specific your inner editor enters and stops your momentum, immediately disregard this rule.

- **WHEN YOU ARE DONE WRITING, FEEL A SENSE OF PRIDE:** The goal of these writing exercises is to fill the page. When you do this, allow yourself to feel proud and revel in the accomplishment. Take it in, savor it, and use the momentum to write again as soon as possible. Do not negate your work or compare it to anyone else's. Negations and comparisons are momentum killers and major steps on the path to writer's block. Of all the rules, this is definitely the most important one.

NOW IT'S TIME TO DO SOME EXERCISES ...

LET'S FACE IT

Some people never forget a face. Perhaps the face you create in this exercise will lead to an unforgettable character, too. Start by circling whatever attributes appeal to you in each section below. Eventually you will start to picture a face. Once that happens, let the emerging image dictate the rest of your choices.

FACE SHAPE:
round
heart
oval
pear

COMPLEXION/ SKIN TYPE:
ruddy
weatherworn
pitted
smooth
café au lait
freckled
fair
greasy
olive

EYE SHAPE:
almond
beady
bulging
crescent
saucer

EYE COLOR:
brown
hazel
green
blue
black
gray
bloodshot
yellowed

NOSE:
hooked
bulbous
prominent
turned up
broken
button

CHEEKS:
apple
flabby
chubby
hollow
rosy

HAIR COLOR:
black
brown
white
blond
auburn
silver

HAIR TEXTURE:
bouncy
fine
frizzy
oily
stringy
curly
straight

MOUTH/LIPS:
thin
full
ripe
puckered
cruel
protruding
chapped

TEETH:
buck
crooked
yellow
dentures
gapped
pearly
jagged

CHIN/JAW:
cleft chin
double chin
Neanderthal jaw
receding chin
square chin

BLEMISHES AND OTHER FEATURES:
age spots
laugh lines
dimples
acne
scar(s)
birthmark
wart(s)
glasses
heavy cosmetics

It's time to give this person a name:

FIRST: ______________________

MIDDLE: ______________________

LAST: ______________________

NOW COMES THE FUN PART: You get to embody the character you just created and write from his or her point of view. Start with: *No one ever said I was ...*

TAKE THE NEXT STEP

Go back through all the hair texture options above. This time think about your writing and/or your writing practice. Underline the one word that best describes it. Facing the future, would you like to keep this description or would you prefer to give it a makeover or face-lift? What word might you prefer to use? What will you do to best embody this word?

A BUCK A WORD

Close your eyes and let your finger wander over this grid of words. Open your eyes. The word on which your finger landed is the one you will use as the main focus for your next writing. Do this twice—once for each writing area below. In the Take the Next Step section you'll learn how to turn this box of words into a valuable and portable "buck a word" idea generator.

chocolate	quartz	money	muscle	doorknob	temptation	eraser	sandals	martian	moon
bubble	tangerine	blood	dirt	London	junk	thief	hitchhike	crayon	guilt
trick	holiday	upset	isolation	xylophone	glisten	WWII	lilacs	helium	kite
corner	rabies	alligator	gamble	engine	volcano	trigger	knife	onion	elf
cave	lemons	balance	roll	ice cream	chance	Paris	kitten	hump	swirl
snow	whale	oblong	well	appetite	portrait	quiz	photo	zipper	gush
Neptune	shock	dust	termite	lightning	urgency	captain	sardine	igloo	baby
laughing	mango	judge	episode	orangutan	umpteen	hunger	basketball	ginger	solo
diamond	defend	dome	hip	corduroy	orchestra	freight	fighting	orbit	wig
braid	drape	opal	candy	parent	yesterday	victory	chapter	curtain	hail

YOUR WORD:

Start with: *The buccaneer ...*

YOUR WORD:

Start with: *The two bucks ...*

TAKE THE NEXT STEP

Make a copy of the box of words above and cut it out along the thick border. The result is a rectangle of words about the size of a dollar bill. Put it in your wallet, and you will have a wealth of writing ideas with you at all times. You can't beat the price either: 100 words for a buck!

Sbil Dam ∘ One

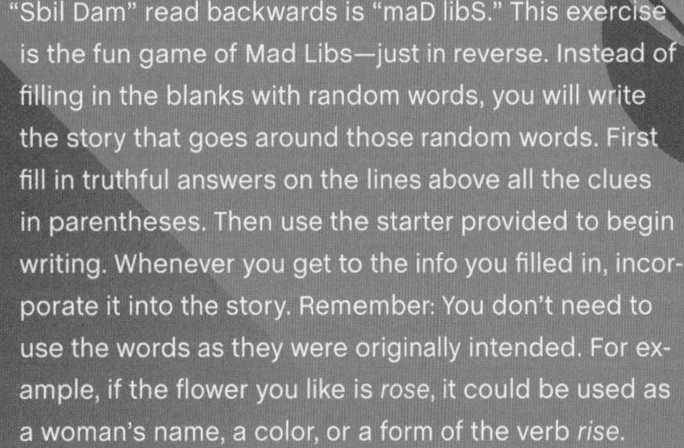

"Sbil Dam" read backwards is "maD libS." This exercise is the fun game of Mad Libs—just in reverse. Instead of filling in the blanks with random words, you will write the story that goes around those random words. First fill in truthful answers on the lines above all the clues in parentheses. Then use the starter provided to begin writing. Whenever you get to the info you filled in, incorporate it into the story. Remember: You don't need to use the words as they were originally intended. For example, if the flower you like is *rose*, it could be used as a woman's name, a color, or a form of the verb *rise*.

I remember when I visited ...

(favorite vacation destination)

(your favorite color)

(first and last name of a relative you like)

(-*ing* verb from a sport you like)

(-*ly* adverb describing how you write)

(three adjectives describing your bedroom)

(a flower you like)

(your favorite candy or candy bar)

(title of a favorite song or movie)

(name of your elementary school)

(a street in your neighborhood)

TAKE THE NEXT STEP

Sbil Dam is fun to do with a partner. Either copy this page or find a friend who also owns this book. Both of you will fill in answers for the clues in parentheses on your own copy. Then swap. Use the starter provided, and whenever you get to the info your partner supplied, put it right into the story. When you are done writing, share what you created with your partner. Return the exercise to its original owner as a souvenir of your writing adventure.

TRY-an-ANGLE

Upon first glance, the shape to the right looks like a triangle. Let your imagination wander as you look at the shape from all sorts of angles and write down a short list of other things it might be. The first ones that came to me were a slice of pizza and an ice cream cone (it says a lot about where my mind is).

Use each and every item you came up with in a story that starts:

The air in the space station was ...

TAKE THE NEXT STEP

Should you ever get stuck, it might help to look at your work from new and different angles. Try reading what you were working on from the bottom to the top, word by word. Or turn it upside down and see which words jump out at you. Or maybe hold it up to a mirror and see which words make the neatest-looking patterns. The oddness and silliness of this exercise will give your mind a chance to take the break it needs. In the process, you will hopefully see things a bit differently and allow the next step to surface. Think of it as turning a frown upside down—with your writing.

You Are Cordially Invited

THE INVITATION WAS

The Invitation was

By changing the type of pen you write with (or the font you always use in your word processing document), your writing mood and vocabulary will also change. In this exercise, you will be using the same starting phrase four different times. Each time, try to write the entire first line in a similar font as the one provided. The rest of the short writing can be in your own handwriting, but try to make the entire paragraph sound like the first line looks.

The Invitation was

THE INVITATION WAS

TAKE THE NEXT STEP

If you are having trouble capturing or maintaining a mood, an atmosphere, or even a character's personality, type the story in a font that encapsulates what you are trying to express. Our brains respond well to visual stimuli, and by turning an abstract (**MOOD**/atmosphere/**personality**) into a tangible font, we are able to perceive it and process it better.

SIMILE BUT DIFFERENT

Pick an item from each column in the chart to create a simile. The odder the simile, the more fun it is to invent a story around. If you want, generate a few similes and use them all. Examples: *crooked like a yo-yo in a debate*; *wild like a rocking chair in sneakers*. Write your simile(s) here:

rotten like	a lead balloon	in pajamas
pink like	mashed potatoes	in headlights
ripe like	a yo-yo	at a wedding
handsome like	a feminist	in handcuffs
crisp like	a pig	in a dentist's chair
tempting like	bricks	in flames
romantic like	a congressman	in a cookie jar
crooked like	a cheerleader	in summer
cold like	a jalopy	in a debate
sharp like	a hillbilly	in a video game
fresh like	a pinch hitter	in sepia tones
snobby like	a bowler	up a creek
wild like	Richard Nixon	in a pocket
hairy like	a dream	in left field
backwards like	dynamite	in the doghouse
stubborn like	a banana split	at a Bar Mitzvah
inflated like	a cockroach	at a protest march
loose like	a geek	in a junkyard
annoying like	eggs	in battle
crazy like	bagels	in a time warp
helpful like	a puppet	in cyberspace
psychic like	a rocking chair	in a think tank
witty like	a diamond	in sneakers
bored like	a cloud	in the refrigerator
clever like	lipstick	in a tornado

TAKE THE NEXT STEP

Similes are comparisons that jazz up your writing. Creative people also tend to be quite adept at another type of comparison: comparing themselves to others, usually those who are more prolific or successful. This is destructive and a waste of time. Instead, take the time to honor who you are. If you want to be more prolific, set aside more writing time. If you want to be more successful, learn how to make your work more professional and polished before you send it out into the world. Change because you want it for yourself, not because you are comparing yourself to, or competing with, someone else.

Use this starting phrase for your story, making sure to include the simile(s) you've created somewhere in the piece.

I took a sip of ...

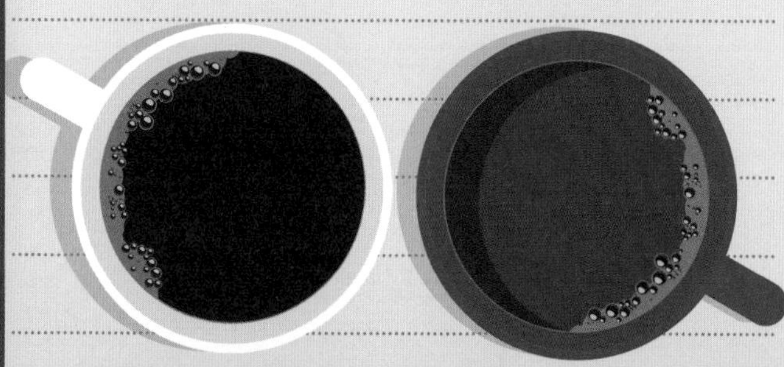

Calli GRAMMES

In a collection of verse titled *Calligrammes*, Guillaume Apollinaire composed poems in the shape of the image they described. In this exercise you are given some very basic shapes in which to write a poem or prose. Make sure the subject matter is linked to the shape. Use the starters provided.

The power of...

Light years from...

Darkened by...

TAKE THE NEXT STEP

Writing comes in many shapes other than books, magazines, newspapers, and movies. One of the shapes my writing takes is in rules for games I invent. I like trying to reach the difficult balance between brevity, clarity, comprehensiveness, and user-friendliness. I also love creating writing exercises and prompts for writers, like the ones in this book. If you've never tried your hand at writing exercises or prompts, I encourage you to give it a try. Then give them to a writer-friend as an idea-sparking gift.

Lingo-istics

Lingo-istics is my term for adding touches of lingo to your dialogue and narrative to make your writing sound more realistic. Here's a chance to try your ear at some lingo-istics.

Pick a number between 1 and 5, and locate it to the right. This is a list of phrases to use in your story.

Start with: *Lately ...*

1. TRUCKER: Big A (Amarillo, Texas); Antler Alley (deer crossing); Wally World (Wal-Mart); Bear in the Air (helicopter police); Big Slab (interstate); Crotch Rocket (motorcycle); Salt Shaker (snow plow); Taking Pictures (police with radar)

2. COP: A&B (assault and battery); FTA (failing to appear for court appearance); SO (sheriff's office); Side B (left side of building); ETOH ON BOARD (intoxicated); BOLO (be on the lookout); ATL (attempt to locate)

3. PRISONER: Dump Truck (lawyer who makes a deal at the expense of clients); Bean Chute (food tray slot); Chalking (running interference while a mate breaks a rule); Badge (correctional officer); Cellie (cellmate); Bo-Bos (sneakers)

4. RESTAURANT: The Pit (dish area); On the Fly (needed ASAP); Campers (party that stays too long); Coupon (cheap customer); Alley Rally (meeting before a shift begins); Hockey Puck (well-done burger); Back of the House (kitchen)

5. AUSTRALIAN: Earbashing (nonstop chatter); Maccas (McDonald's); Daks (trousers); Captain Cook (have a look); Botter (something that is excellent); Aerial Ping-Pong (Australian rules football); Seppo (an American)

TAKE THE NEXT STEP

Can you write a thirty-second radio commercial to sell a remedy for writer's block? Make sure you use lots of writer's lingo to show that you relate to and understand the craft, as well as the challenges. Write a commercial that would make you want to buy the remedy, too.

Hey, You!

In the second-person point of view, you use the pronoun *you*. Writing from this POV is a bit of a stretch at first, but once you get used to it, it can be really effective and fun. A good way to learn how to use the second person is to teach readers how to do something.

Choose a title from the list below. Use the second person (you) to teach your readers how to do something. Start with, *First you...*

- How to Miss a Bus
- How to Have a Pet Adopt You
- How to Find a Needle in a Haystack
- How to Almost Meet a Celebrity
- How to Boil Water
- How to Say You're Sorry
- How to Meddle in Someone Else's Affairs

TAKE THE NEXT STEP

How-to books are wonderful, but the best advice is whatever works best for you. For example: Some writing books tell you it's best to create an outline before writing. Perhaps you write best by letting the story flow from you and then going back and editing without ever creating an outline. If your approach is working, ignore the advice from the experts, and don't feel like you're doing something wrong. However, if your approach isn't working, try options from as many experts, writing colleagues, and friends as possible until you find the how-to that works best for you.

1.

Pick two numbers between 1 and 30, and locate them in the grid below. These are two two-word starters.

You will do two timed two-minute writings, one with each starter you chose. The writings do not have to be linked. The goal is for you to see how much you can actually write in two minutes. Now write!

1 The captain	7 She quoted	13 The aroma	19 After confessing	25 His first
2 The license	8 The dice	14 I suspected	20 Letting go	26 Without thinking
3 He dialed	9 At dusk	15 Six students	21 Hanging from	27 The flames
4 The judge	10 The visitor	16 While underground	22 He vowed	28 She blabbed
5 The fox	11 The lullaby	17 I voted	23 Her perfurme	29 My stomach
6 Disguised as	12 The cliff	18 By nightfall	24 The printout	30 Yellow flowers

TAKE THE NEXT STEP

In just two minutes you can make notes for a future writing, add a sentence or two to a current writing to keep the momentum going and your mind on the piece, or choose another two-word starter and write for two minutes. By doing this you'll feel great because, even though life is hectic, you are still honoring your pledge to stick to a writing practice. You will also make sure your muse knows you are truly committed to your writing. It's amazing how you can turn what otherwise would have been a frustration about not having enough time into a positive asset to your practice ... in just two minutes. Attitude is just as important as other facets of writing. Seeing yourself in a committed light is a big boost.

2.

SIDEWAYS GLANCE →

Sometimes writing in a different direction changes how you write. Try it! Start with: *I couldn't help staring ...*

TAKE THE NEXT STEP

Stretch your peripheral vision by looking as far to the right and left as you can without moving your head. Describe what might be just beyond your line of vision.

Stretching our eyes, minds, legs, and hearts is very helpful to developing our writing muscles!

Gems

Use the words as you get to them. Start with:

I plucked the ______________________________ from ...

sparkling sapphire

blinded by a diamond

ruby red

aquamarine

precious

black pearls

TAKE THE NEXT STEP

Unusual sensory combinations spark readers' imaginations and send them to places they normally wouldn't go on their own. Here are two: the smell of a joke, the taste of a territory. Come up with some of your own to use in future writings.

basement

Picture a basement or cellar from your childhood. Mentally open the door, descend the stairs, feel the banister, take in the smells. Notice the quality of light and what's on the steps, floor, and walls. Hear the sound of the pipes and the other noises. Behind a hot water heater, in the shadows, is something you never noticed before ... an old wooden door! You go to it, twist the knob in your hand ... Now start writing!

TAKE THE NEXT STEP

If you were to host a writing party in a cellar or basement, what snacks, events, entertainment, and parting gifts would you supply to keep it thematic? Other than your muse, who else might you invite?

CATCH-UP № 1

Finish the story. Start with: *The first time I saw him, he was digging ketchup out of a bottle with a knife ...*

TAKE THE NEXT STEP

Dig deeper into the main character in this story. What does he or she really care about? What motivates him or her? How is he or she like you?

CATCH-UP № 2

Finish the story. Start with: *The first time I saw her, she was teaching third graders that ketchup is a vegetable ...*

TAKE THE NEXT STEP

Do you believe writing is:

- teachable?
- something you're born with?
- learned only by doing?
- genetic?

What is your opinion about teaching or learning writing? How does this affect the way you approach your craft?

States of Mind

Use the map shape if you choose. Finish the story. Start with: *I was in a California state of mind yet stuck on a farm in Iowa ...*

TAKE THE NEXT STEP

State a fear that keeps you from writing your personal truth. Let go of the fear a little bit every time you write. Don't jump off the high wire without a net. Take it nice and easy by simply letting go of a little more fear with each writing session.

VOCAL-EYES ONE

Finish the story. Start with: *I met her voice before I met her eyes ...*

TAKE THE NEXT STEP

Finding your writing voice is important. Go through this exercise and circle words and phrases that could have only been generated by your voice. Go back and identify more throughout this book.

VOCAL-EYES TWO

Finish the story. Start with: *I met his eye long before I heard that familiar voice ...*

TAKE THE NEXT STEP

Do you confuse which and that? Here's an easy rule: Choose the one that sounds right. And here's a technical one: that introduces restrictive clauses, as in *I'm looking for the book that I heard reviewed on NPR yesterday.* Which introduces nonrestrictive clauses: *The book, which had a magnificent cover, was lost forever.* Go back through your exercises and make corrections.

DOUBLE AGENT

Write using the starter. Whatever word you write when you first come to the brackets, you must use every time you come to another set of brackets on the rest of the page. Start with: *He's my brother, but he's also a double agent ...*

TAKE THE NEXT STEP

Double your productivity by making your goals quantifiable. "Write every day" is easier to achieve when it is worded "Write ten minutes a day, three days a week for three months."

Record two quantifiable writing goals to accomplish in the next two days.

DECEMBERSERK

FINISH THE STORY. *There is no one more berserk than .... on Christmas Eve.*

TAKE THE NEXT STEP

Shop through your December memories and make a list of six. Use these to prompt further writings.

SEPTember

Use these seven words:

SEPTic **SEPTuplet** **SEPTuagenarian** **SEPTillion** **SEPTennial** **SEPTilateral** **SEPTum**

Start with: *We took separate ...*

TAKE THE NEXT STEP

Separate seven memories from the Septembers of your life and note them here. Use these to prompt further writings.

1 # April Fools

2

The greatest practical joke I ever played used a computer shareware software program called LAVA, which turned the monitor into a series of oozing and flowing colors. I installed it on a technophobic friend's brand-new first computer. You should have seen the look of terror on his face! Write about a prank you've pulled or one that someone has pulled on you.

Start with: *I wish you could have ...*

8 9

15 16

TAKE THE NEXT STEP

List six pranks or other April memories from your life. Use these to prompt further writings.

Write about a teacher or mentor you've had. Use as many adjectives and descriptive phrases as you can—to excess, even! Start with: *Most teachers have eyes in the back of their heads, but ...*

TAKE THE NEXT STEP

There's a lesson in everything, including regrets. List one regret you have in the area of writing. Now turn this into an uplifting lesson by focusing on one positive facet: *I am proud of ...*

TWO Coats

Use these words in your story:

roller *brush* *paint* *spackle* *coveralls*

Start with: *My first coat that wasn't a hand-me-down ...*

TAKE THE NEXT STEP

Do you see (creative) writing as a luxury or a necessity? Why? How does this point of view help or hurt your writing practice?

TRUTH or DARE

Think about a personal truth that very few people know. Now write down the ultimate dare to which you'd be willing to subject yourself in order to keep this truth a secret. Write the dare here. »

For this story you are now a being in the year 3030 named RoTon. Write from RoTon's point of view, making sure to incorporate the aforementioned dare somewhere in the piece. Start with: *The lights went twink and the carrialet began to ...*

TAKE THE NEXT STEP

Think of something you have now because you dared to overcome obstacles in the past. That experience sure looks different in hindsight, doesn't it? Write a lesson you learned that can help overcome one of your current creative obstacles.

PEEPHOLE ONE

You look through the peephole of your front door and see this eyeball. →

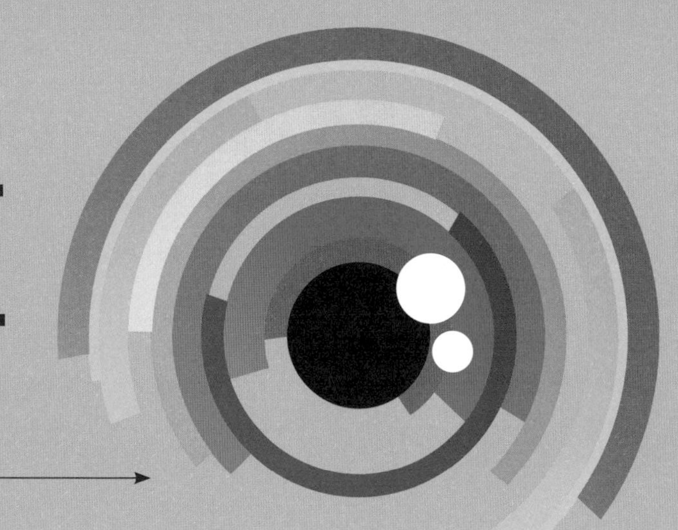

Play out the story. Start with: *I'm a bit of a ...*

TAKE THE NEXT STEP

If you could look through a peephole into the future and see one of your completed writing projects, which project would you want to see, and what would it look like? Be specific. Do something today to move this project forward.

Zounds of Sounds

Use the sounds as you come to them. Start with: *The guru told us to ...*

tick tock

chime

crash

pin drop

tinkling

thud

boing

shhhh!

scratching

TAKE THE NEXT STEP

If you were a creative writing guru, what daily practice would you make mandatory for your devotees so they might become the best possible writers?

Do you currently practice what you preach? Why or why not?

RESOLUTION REVOLUTION

Use each letter as you get to it. Start with: *New Year's resolutions make me ...*

N

E

W

Y

E

A

R

S

R

E

S

O

L U

T

I

O

N

TAKE THE NEXT STEP

New Year's resolutions are passé. Think New Day resolutions instead. What new writing-related thing do you resolve to do in the next twenty-four hours?

REMEMBER ME?

This is a personal ad from a local newspaper.

CHRIS—LAST TUES, 8:45 P.M.—BOOK BIN CAFÉ. Want to thank you again for the cappuccino. You made my day. Haven't been able to get you off my mind, especially your hair. Went back three times to look for you. Kicking myself for not asking for your phone number. P.O. Box 8281.

Write how the scenario unfolds. Start with: I don't usually …

TAKE THE NEXT STEP

List those who have helped or influenced you on your path to becoming a successful writer.

Send each individual a note of thanks. It'll make them feel good and keep you serious about your craft. (Thanks to Teresa Piccari, writing instructor and creativity coach, for this exercise idea.)

Invisible Ink

1. Find a blank sheet of paper and place it over the paper image below.

2. Grab a ballpoint pen. No gels, markers, or roller balls for this one.
3. Slowly and methodically—pushing down super-duper hard—write on the top sheet (in ALL CAPS) one thing you want to accomplish with your writing this month.
4. Throw away the top paper.
5. Mark your calendar exactly thirty days from today to remind yourself to come back to this page. When you return in a month, follow the directions in the Take the Next Step section.

TAKE THE NEXT STEP

Welcome back. I hope you had a great month. Please locate a soft-lead, dark no. 2 pencil. A nonmechanical pencil is best. Hold the pencil at an angle and gently shade over the paper image area above. Your message from one month ago will magically appear. If you haven't yet accomplished what you intended, there's still plenty of time. Start today. If you did accomplish it, congratulations! Now create a goal for the next month. By the way, with this exercise being the exception, it's always best to keep your goals visible rather than invisible.

WHO, WHAT, WHEN, WHERE ... AND WHY NOT?

WHO:	WHAT:	WHEN:	WHERE:	EXPRESSION:
A KING	A CHAIN	DAYBREAK	AN ISLAND	"WHY NOT?"

Use these five items in a story. Start with: *It's hard to believe, but ...*

TAKE THE NEXT STEP

For whom do you write? Describe your mental picture of your audience. Find a picture—via an online image search, a magazine, or perhaps a photo you took—that depicts the mental image of your audience giving you a standing ovation. Place it in this book to help you stay clear and motivated about your commitment to writing.

MUTE BUTTON

Use as many of the following in your story as you can:

Volume	02	Up	Record
Channel	Control	Select	Down
59	15	Remote	Source
Last	Favorite	67	HDMI

Start with: *If the mute button worked on people, I'd ...*

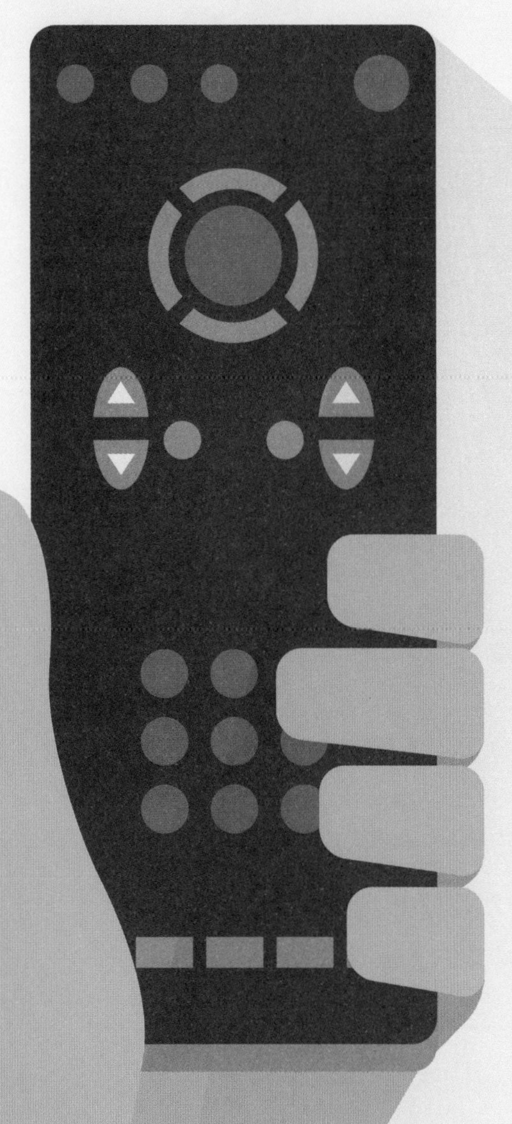

TAKE THE NEXT STEP

Find a picture of a stop sign and keep it at your desk. The next time your inner critic tries to tamper with your creativity, hold up the stop sign. This action should immediately mute that destructive voice.

HODGE PODGE

Write the name of a neighbor from your childhood: __________

Write an expression that a friend overuses: __________

Write a relative's odd personality quirk: __________

Write a physical attribute you wish you had: __________

This is now *your* name, an expression *you* overuse, *your* personality quirk, and *your* physical attribute. Write in the first person from this perspective. Start with: *Not to burst your bubble ...*

TAKE THE NEXT STEP

If you could put your name plus one word describing your writer-self inside a clear bubble that will travel the globe and be seen by millions, what would that one word be? (If you're having trouble, list many words and eliminate some daily.)

WANNA WRITE?

On this page, write all the topics you'd like to write about today (or someday). Separate each topic with a comma and fill all the lines on the page. Be as outrageous as you like. Go over the edge! Approach this with the attitude that the sky's the limit!

TAKE THE NEXT STEP

Did you ever want to be someone else? If you could be any writer, dead or alive, who would you choose, and why? What one trait from this person can you incorporate into your writing practice?

ODE TO A SEASON

Here's a chance to roast your least favorite season. Write in second tense (*you*). As an example, here is a first line about my least favorite season, summer: *Although you are lauded by most, I despise your pea-soup breath that strangles like an assassin's noose.*

Ode to...

TAKE THE NEXT STEP

If your writing practice were a garden, what would it look like? Be honest! In keeping with the garden theme, what's one new way you can tend to your writing that you've never tried before? Do it!

Daydreamer

Finish the story. Start with: While the teacher lectured, I stared out the window ...

TAKE THE NEXT STEP

Describe a window you remember using to daydream. Not the view—the actual window.

Now imagine you are there. Daydream and stare out that "mind window" for a few minutes. What did you see? What did you dream?

SHAKE-SPEAR

Use all these words that were coined by the Bard:

ARCH-VLLAIN   MADCAP   GALLANTRY   TRIPPINGLY   PAGEANTRY

Start with: *He laid his right hand on the spear ...*

TAKE THE NEXT STEP

"A friendly eye could never see such faults." —William Shakespeare

Instead of asking for critiques as we are trained to do, give friends or colleagues a piece of your writing and ask them to point out three positive things to you. The praise will feel good, and it will motivate you to write more.

Haunted Castle

You've been invited to spend a night at a haunted castle. List the top six things you'd pack:

1.

2.

3.

4.

5.

6.

Use them all in a story. Start with: *Sometimes glamour ...*

TAKE THE NEXT STEP

If you had to pack up quickly and leave your home, would you grab any of your writing? If so, which pieces? If not, what do you need to do to get your writing on this priority list?

QUACK?

Write down six animal sounds, like *moo*, *baa*, *quack*, etc.

Use as many of these sounds as you can in a story starting with: *Some relationships are better than others ...*

TAKE THE NEXT STEP

To prevent ruining a relationship when asked to critique someone's writing, always offer specific constructive advice for each critique you address. Practice by critiquing a specific thing in the writing on this page. Now offer yourself a constructive way to change it.

Memory Lane

Take a few short trips down memory lane. Write the truth, embellished memories, or complete fiction! Use the starting phrases to get you moving down the path.

I remember learning ...

___

I remember biting ...

___

I remember the balloons ...

___

I remember falling ...

___

TAKE THE NEXT STEP

The phrase "I remember" often takes us back to childhood, where we learned using all our senses, especially touch and taste. Finish this: *I remember the taste o*
Tomorrow, before you do anything else, finish this: *I remember the smell of ...*

DOUBLE TROUBLE

All these words have two (or more) meanings. Use each word at least twice, one for each definition:

light	check	bat	press	pen	ring	fly
plug	club	note	band	can	date	sink

Start with: *The trouble with ...*

TAKE THE NEXT STEP

What do the writing monsters that trouble you (who perhaps live under your desk) look like?

Instead of slaying them, what can you do to befriend the monsters and use them to your advantage?

CIRCLE GAME•ONE

Circle the one word that most appeals to you:

attitude
blueberry
carousel
dungeon
eggs

Circle another word that appeals to you:

flashlight
garage
handsome
insensitive
jumbled

Circle yet another word you find appealing:

keepsake
lemonade
melon
nonsense
outfield

Use these three words in a story. Start with: *Sometimes I feel just like a gerbil, running around and around on his wheel!*

TAKE THE NEXT STEP

In terms of a writing practice, what type of gerbil are you?

1. Do you run round and round on a wheel?
2. Do you avoid the wheel?
3. Are you fearful of leaving the wheel?
4. Do you run freely without need of a wheel?

If a writing practice was an airplane instead of a gerbil's wheel, what would you do differently?

REBUS REBUTTAL

Instead of words, this exercise has pictures. Use them as you come to them.
Start with: *After the debate, the underdog candidate ...*

TAKE THE NEXT STEP

What if writer's block was a word game in which you had to put words into blocks of preset patterns to form a shape poem?

Use this example to try it on your own.

BAKER'S DOZEN

Use these thirteen foods and food-related phrases in your story:

- sweet potato
- that's how the cookie crumbles
- whipped cream
- persimmon
- flat as a pancake
- shrimp cocktail
- steak
- passion fruit
- chocolate
- cool as a cucumber
- chicken
- ice cubes
- red as a beet

Start with: *She dipped ...*

TAKE THE NEXT STEP

There are lots of ways to feed your writer-self. I like to read. And, breaking a writing rule, I am okay reading a similar genre to what I am in the process of writing. What writing rules have you broken? What writing rules do you abide by?

REMINISCING ¤ ONE

Imagine talking to a friend from your childhood. Retell stories and reminisce about favorite times. Use the starting phrases provided.

Do you remember the time we tried ...

Do you remember the time we called ...

Do you remember the time we asked ...

Do you remember the time we joined ...

TAKE THE NEXT STEP

Positive self-talk is a great way to achieve goals. Create a writing goal. (No negative words, please.)

Every morning and evening, repeat it aloud to yourself. You *can* make it happen.

PHOTO OP

Although the famous saying states that "a picture is worth a thousand words," for this exercise you need only write as many words as your hands can crank out in ten minutes. Pick a number between 1 and 5, and locate it below. This is the picture you will use to spark your writing.

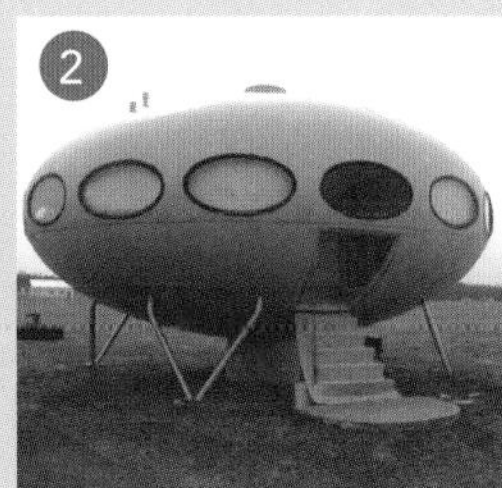

If you need an extra push to get started, use this to begin your writing: *Entering ...*

TAKE THE NEXT STEP

Everyone has heard of a photo op, but what about a writing connection op? It's an occasion that puts you in front of someone who can help you take your creative process to the next level. Here is but one of many examples: Join a local writing group that has a yearly conference. Tell the conference committee you'd be happy to drive or escort presenters (authors, agents, editors) to and from the airport, bus stop, restaurants, etc. By doing this, you will get quality time with professionals who have successfully navigated the land of writing. Don't barrage them with questions; instead, enjoy casual conversation and, if you have a natural opportunity to talk about your writing, do so. The key is to connect and bond so you can perhaps continue the connection.

Ship Shape

Write until you fill in the entire shape. There are no lines; therefore you can be creative and free as the wind. Start with: *The ship's sail...*

TAKE THE NEXT STEP

When in need of perking up, some folks go boating, some play board games, and others listen to loud music. List four things you do.

The next time you are lethargic, do one of these to perk up before returning to your writing with renewed energy.

High Ryes

Finish the story. Start with: *The building where the bakery from my childhood used to be ...*

TAKE THE NEXT STEP

Money is definitely a motivator. Other than making some dough, however, what are some direct and indirect benefits you get from writing? Remind yourself of these often.

decisions

Use the words on the page as you get to them. Start with: *Unless things change ...*

either

or

if

then

TAKE THE NEXT STEP

What are the top three things you do to avoid writing?

1. ____________________

2. ____________________

3. ____________________

Make a decision to *not* do one of them for an entire week and write instead. Start ... now!

ambidextrous

Use your nondominant hand to write this exercise. Even if it feels odd and uncomfortable, stick with it! The lines are spread out to help you. Start with: *I remember my first ...*

TAKE THE NEXT STEP

What was the first compliment you remember receiving about your writing? From whom? Do you remember what you had written? How did it affect your future writings?

DOUBLE DARE

Finish the story. Start with: *She said, "I double dare you ..."*

TAKE THE NEXT STEP

Name one thing you've done that others might interpret as daring or risky but that you see as merely a path to a solution or a determined part of your process. How often do you take on such "risks"? Would you be happier if you did them more or less often? Make that happen.

Soft Spoken

Finish the story. Start with: *She whispered ...*

UN-MORAL • ONE

Use the "un-moral" at the bottom of the page to conclude the story you are about to write. Start with: *She was not a ...*

The Un-Moral: It's best to count your chickens before they're hatched.

TAKE THE NEXT STEP

Quantify what you've written in the last week. Use whatever works best: word count, number of pages, hours spent writing, etc.

- Your number:__________________.
- Set a new, larger, quantifiable writing goal for next week: ______________________.

Check back at the end of the week and applaud yourself, whether you achieved it or not. Setting a goal is a big accomplishment in and of itself.

BAN-THE-BLANK-PAGE BRIGADE

Here's an army of starting phrases whose sole purpose is to help you combat fear of the blank page. The irony of using them is that you must start with a blank sheet of paper. So grab one. Speak the phrases aloud as you copy them one by one onto your paper. At some point you'll hit one that you will want to explore further. Often it's not the phrase you just wrote but one you transcribed a few minutes earlier. Rewrite that phrase and see where your pen takes you as you fill the rest of the page.

- Her skirt spun around her like a ...
- Hidden inside a slice of carrot cake ...
- Holding on for dear life ...
- Holding the baby for the first time ...
- I admit I was a bit jealous of ...
- I bit my tongue and ...
- I broke into the piggy bank and ...
- I didn't plan on returning ...
- I don't care what anyone says, I ...
- I had butterflies in my stomach ...
- I remember sitting on Santa's lap and asking ...
- I took out my Czech-English, English-Czech dictionary and ...
- I was never chosen ...
- I wrote my initials in the dust on ...
- If we go on strike ...
- In every school photo I ...
- In the corner hung ...
- In the middle of the cave ...
- In the rock she saw the face of ...
- It was an ear-piercing ...
- Knowing his ulterior motive ...
- Last I heard, he was hiding in the ...
- Listening to the rain ...
- Margie wrote "Return to Sender" on the envelope and ...
- My blind date last weekend looked a lot like ...
- New grass under my bare feet ...
- No matter how you do the math, it ...
- On the surface nothing seemed different, yet ...
- One afternoon while collecting beach glass ...
- Right after the twenty-first hour at the silent retreat ...
- She called out to him ...
- She left the scent of coconuts in her wake and whenever she ...
- She was the one in the bright-orange sneakers ...
- Shortly after I met Igor ...
- The black satchel in the middle of the road ...
- The dance instructor took ...
- The foam of the waves ...

TAKE THE NEXT STEP

A bucket brigade (human chain) is a way to transport items by passing them from one stationary person to the next. Its most famous use was by firefighters who passed buckets to each other when extinguishing a blaze. You can use the same concept to accomplish your writing goals. Figure out who in your community (local or virtual) can help you with each stage of your process. Line them up (figuratively), and with their support you will accomplish your goal. People love to help—so let them!

Here Ye Here Ye

Start with: Here ye sits and thinks if only ye had something to write, ye would be in a state of delight. And so ye begins, with a dip of the quill ...

TAKE THE NEXT STEP

Describe a writing session when you thought you had nothing to write, weren't in the mood to write, or your muse was in hiding, yet you were very prolific.

Remember this the next time you think you've got writer's block.

STOP WRITE LISTEN

Begin with the starting phrase provided. Write until you get to the STOP sign. Even if you are in the middle of a word, sentence, or thought, STOP! Begin writing with the next starting phrase. Write from your heart. Be honest!

Start now:

When I face a blank page, I feel ...

STOP

What I really want to write is ...

TAKE THE NEXT STEP

Compose a permission slip, giving yourself permission to write what you want, even if it feels scary. The next time you sit down to write (or now), start writing what you really want to write.

Tooth Fairy

You are a disgruntled tooth fairy. You can't understand why Santa and even the Easter Bunny get more attention than you do. You just visited twins who expected $20 per tooth. Start with: *I can't believe ...*

TAKE THE NEXT STEP

Characters often live beyond one piece of writing. Write something that will happen in the future to one of the characters in your story as a result of this writing.

Do this with a character who has stuck with you from another writing.

HANDS DOWN/FEET UP

Put down your pen for a minute. Close your eyes and with your nonwriting hand explore the hand you usually write with. Notice the calluses, rough spots, scars, nails, knuckles, skin texture, and so on. Think of the many experiences you've had using this hand. Pick one of these experiences, and write about it. Start with: *I felt ...*

Now take off your shoes and close your eyes. With both hands, explore your feet. Notice how different they feel from your hands. Think of the many places your feet have been. Pick one of those, and write about it. Start with: *I knew ...*

TAKE THE NEXT STEP

Your body holds many stories. Jot down two stories that your knees might tell. How about your chin?

The next time you're looking for something to write, choose one of these stories.

Peculiar Pet

Pick one of these peculiar pets:

- a hoarse giraffe
- a neurotic ape
- a twenty-pound mouse
- a hummingbird that is afraid of heights
- a cat that is allergic to other cats
- a tiger with an ingrown toenail
- a cockroach that is afraid of the dark
- a five-legged goat
- a deaf rooster

You are now this pet. Write using its voice and point of view. Tell us your name, where you came from, what you do all day, and how your new owner has reacted to owning you. Start with: *The folks at the ...*

TAKE THE NEXT STEP

Write an ad proclaiming why you, as a writer, would make the best candidate to adopt a four-hundred-pound turtle. Really make yourself sound good.

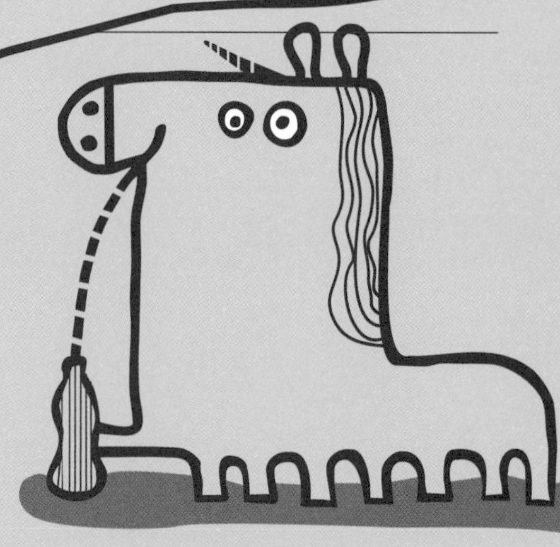

CONGRATS

Write a letter congratulating yourself on something you did especially well today. Perhaps you stayed on your diet, or avoided someone who usually gives you grief, or took procrastination to a new high, or completed this exercise!

Dear __________________________,

I commend you on the fine job you did today ...

TAKE THE NEXT STEP

Write your ideal job description; that is, one that uses all your talents, pays extraordinarily well, and allows you to wake up happy every day.

Sometimes just putting it out into the universe will make it happen. (Be careful what you ask for!)

IT'S ALL IN YOUR HEAD

Congratulations on your new job writing for an upstart supermarket tabloid. Unfortunately, you have a limited budget for travel and resources. This means your responsibility is to write feature articles based on headlines provided by your boss. All you have in your office is a desk, a chair, a pen, paper, and a wastebasket. There's no computer, no smartphone, no dictionary, no almanac, no nothing. When you ask your boss how you're supposed to do research, he replies, "Everything you need is already in your head. Write from there." He then takes off for parts unknown to gather more headlines for you.

Choose from the provided headlines for today's feature story. Then take your boss's advice and "write from your head."

1. Woman Born with Bird Wings Takes Flight
2. Medical Students Dissecting Corpse Find Watermelon Growing in Stomach
3. Boy with Static Electricity Disease Sparks Major Fire
4. Methane from World's Largest Cow Single-Handedly Increasing Global Warming
5. Flute-Playing Mermaid Spotted in Midtown Manhattan Practicing Scales

TAKE THE NEXT STEP

Years ago people would go to the doctor, describe their symptoms, and get the diagnosis "It's all in your head." When it comes to aches and pains associated with writing, it's often *all in your neck, back, or shoulders*. A chiropractor taught me a great exercise to help relieve these symptoms and improve posture. It's called Wall Angels because it is a standing variation of making snow angels. Here's how to do it: Stand flat against a wall with your feet shoulder-width apart. Gently press your lower back against the wall. Place the back of your elbows, forearms, and wrists against the wall. Bring your arms up and down slowly in an arc while making sure to keep your elbows in contact with the wall. Repeat ten times. It really works!

state fair

Finish the story. Start with: *The best summer of my life was the one when Aunt Nan came to stay for three weeks, and at the state fair my ...*

TAKE THE NEXT STEP

What's your relationship with your writing? Are you a wicked stepmother, a caring aunt, a little brother, an overprotective father, or something else? Describe it. If you'd prefer a different relationship, describe that one. Now do something to nurture this new relationship.

FOLLOWING DIRECTIONS

Use the directional words as you get to them. Start with: ***Just like the little red caboose*** ...

UP

RIGHT

LEFT

DOWN

TAKE THE NEXT STEP

The Little Engine That Could said, "I think I can, I think I can." Write down a facet of your writing craft that would be aided by repeating, "I know I can, I know I can."

Say it over and over until you believe you can. Then do it.

UN-MORAL * TWO

Use the un-moral at the bottom of the page to conclude the story you are about to write. Start with: *The beads of sweat ...*

And the un-moral of the story is:
Every clown has a silver lining.

TAKE THE NEXT STEP

Describe some tears your inner clown wanted to cry but didn't or couldn't. Use these feelings next time you sit down to write.

Wet 'n' Wild

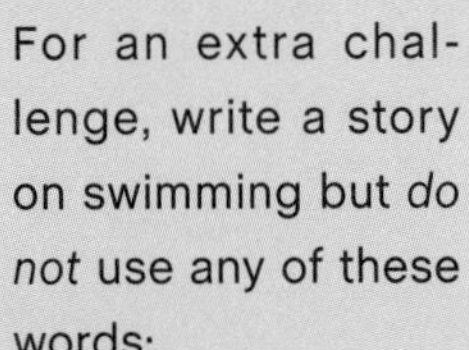

For an extra challenge, write a story on swimming but *do not* use any of these words:

waves

pond

pool

ocean

stream

wet

swim

liquid

water

drink

flow

float

creek

deep

Start with: *Like a fish, I spent my summer ...*

TAKE THE NEXT STEP

Of all the words you were not allowed to use in the story, which one describes your writer-self? Why? Do you want this word to be pertinent a year from now as well? If not, what other word would you like? Why?

Sincerely Yours

Start with: *Dear Dolores, I know it has been thirty-seven years since I have been in touch ...*

TAKE THE NEXT STEP

If you currently have a goal to meet (if you don't, set one right now), go to an online greeting card site. Send a timed e-greeting of congratulations to yourself, scheduled to arrive on the deadline for the goal. Knowing you sent the card will keep you on track. If you prefer to do it the old-fashioned way, give a stamped card to a friend to mail to you two days before your goal deadline.

PAINT THE TOWN PINK

Use the starting phrase and fill the page.
Start with: *When I am in a neon-pink mood ...*

TAKE THE NEXT STEP

Get out a marker or pen in your favorite color and, using proofreader's marks, mark up the writing on this page. Now that your inner editor has had a chance to come out and play, politely tell him it's time to go home. When this book is open, there's no room on the table for him.

A Forkful of Spoonerisms

W.A. Spooner was an English clergyman noted for accidentally transposing sounds within words and phrases. An example of a Spoonerism is saying *crooks and nannies* when you intended to say *nooks and crannies*. Your challenge is to use a pair of Spoonerisms as bookends for a timed writing. In the above example, you would start with *The nooks and crannies ...*, write to fill the page, and conclude your piece with the words *... the crooks and nannies.*

Pick a pair of Spoonerism bookends.

The cozy little nook ... → ... the nosey little cook.

I was lighting a fire ... → ... I was fighting a liar.

Because of a pack of lies ... → ... because of a lack of pies.

It's pouring with rain ... → ... it's roaring with pain.

Save the whales ... → ... wave the sails.

TAKE THE NEXT STEP

If you were to mix four spoonfuls, forkfuls, or other measurable ingredients together to create a recipe for creative juices, what would yours include? Here's mine: a forkful of inspiration; a pinch of perspiration; a dollop of laughter; a heaping tablespoon of royalties. Make sure you take a sip or a gulp of your creative juices every day to keep your momentum going.

OBJECT-IFYING

Writing prompts are all around us. Within eyeshot are many objects that can be used to trigger writings. Out of the corner of my left eye, I see a mug from a local café that has a dangling tea bag string. From this one item, a couple of writings that come to mind are: meeting a blind date at a café but going up to the wrong person (who is also waiting to meet a blind date), and a tent-camping trip in a blizzard that included a visit to a great tea shop.

Choose an object from the list, and shape your writing around it. These objects are intentionally nondescript so your imagination can bring them to life.

1. A Styrofoam cup
2. A flashlight
3. A magnifying glass
4. An old dial telephone
5. A camera
6. A letter
7. A piece of music
8. A calculator
9. A bottle of pills
10. A date book

Use any of the following starters for your writing:

I wonder ...
I worry ...
He wandered ...
He waited ...
She worshipped ...
She wiped ...

TAKE THE NEXT STEP

Where you write is a very personal choice. Perhaps you are most productive when you go to different cafés, sit wherever there's a seat, and tolerate background noise. Or maybe you need your chair, in your home, with your favorite music, your beverage in your favorite cup, and your stuff in view. No matter where you fall in the spectrum, it's important to have a place or space where you know you will be able to write. Wherever it is, no matter how transitory, use personal objects to make it your own for the time you are there.

My Summer Vacation

When telling the stories of your life, there's a lot of freedom in writing about what you haven't done! Use the starting phrase and fill the page.

This past summer I didn't ...

TAKE THE NEXT STEP

This past summer I didn't sleep under a full moon, get up the nerve to wear a bathing suit, or play the penny slot machines—although I had expected to do all of them. If you were a betting person and could envision your writing practice as a slot machine, would you bet more money that you will keep up your writing practice or more money that you will abandon it? Why? If you had to bet in favor of keeping up your practice, how much would you risk?

FUN & GAMES ONE

Use each word in the left column in the line in which it appears. Start with: *I remember that game we used to play ...*

WAR

BALDERDASH

HORSESHOES

MARBLES

TAG

SPIT

TAKE THE NEXT STEP

If you met up with your playful three-year-old self, what one question do you think he or she would ask you about your writing? What's your answer?

WHAT IF?

Write a story to answer this partial question. *What if, at will, people could grow ...*

TAKE THE NEXT STEP

If you could put a dollar value on your current writing assets plus your untapped writing potential, how much would they be worth? What can you do to protect this investment? What can you do to grow it?

NOW WE'RE COOKIN'

Today you will write a recipe for how to get someone to write every day. Don't forget to include a list of ingredients and step-by-step instructions. In lieu of a picture of the completed dish, you will use personal anecdotes and writing samples to demonstrate your point.

Even though you are writing about writing, you will be using words found in actual cooking recipes. Pick a number between 1 and 5, and locate it below. This is a list of words you must use in your "How to Write Every Day" recipe.

1. sauté, quarter, cup, roll, sprinkle, dollop, whisk
2. stir, mix, chop, drain, boil, tablespoon, dissolve
3. simmer, steam, slice, pound, melt, toss, heat
4. grease, roast, fold, rub, cook, bake, tender, shake
5. spoon, blend, season, grind, peel, mince, press

TAKE THE NEXT STEP

Editing is like skimming the fat off the top of the pot of soup. Just like you don't want to put excess fat in your body, you don't want to leave extraneous words, sentences, paragraphs, and chapters in your writing. Hopefully this visual will make it easier to go back to a piece and trim the fat (edit), thereby improving it dramatically. Try your hand at trimming this exercise or another piece of writing.

COMFORT FOODS

ICE CREAM
MACARONI AND CHEESE
MASHED POTATOES
CREAM OF WHEAT
CHICKEN NOODLE SOUP

Use all of these foods in a piece that begins: *He always looked uncomfortable ...*

TAKE THE NEXT STEP

No need to feel uncomfortable if you're not a good speller. To learn that *alright* and *alot* are not words, remember: It's all right to use your dictionary (or spell-checker) a lot. For easy referral, list correct versions of some of your spelling challenges on a sheet in your writing area.

FIRST GRADE

You are a first grader. Write from this perspective. Be inventive and playful! Give yourself a name with these initials:

E________________ T________________ F________________

A nickname: Eye color:

Hair color: Favorite food:

Siblings' ages and names:

How you treat your siblings:

How your siblings treat you:

Thoughts on school:

Thoughts on recess:

Start with: *Here I am, the first day of first grade ...*

TAKE THE NEXT STEP

In pursuit of goals and life passions, at some point we all fail. It's part of the process. Without these experiences we'd never appreciate our accomplishments, discover our strengths, or know who our real friends are. List one such experience and what you learned from it.

Swamp Thing

Finish the story. Start with: *Down by the swamp ...*

TAKE THE NEXT STEP

Set a writing deadline now and ask a core support group to check in regularly with you. We're all swamped, but almost everyone can find time to text, leave a voice message, or send an e-mail. Tell them exactly what to say so it's a mindless task. Example: "Hi. Checking in to make sure you're on track and to let you know I'm here if you have any challenges."

Famous Firsts—One

Finish the story. Start with: *We had spent the afternoon in a café on the Rue Saint-Jacques, a spring afternoon just like any other.* (This first line is from *A Certain Smile* by Francoise Sagan.)

TAKE THE NEXT STEP

When you become rich and famous, what's the first charity you'll make a donation to?

Get out a check right now, fill in the amount you plan to give, sign it, and then write *VOID* over the signature. Keep it by your desk as a reminder of one of the ways your success can and will help others.

SUMMER Better Than Others

Finish the story.

Even though he is my best friend, there are some things he says that drive me nuts. Every June 30, when the year is half over, he always says, "Six of one, half dozen of another." It was clever when we were nine, but now it makes me want to ...

TAKE THE NEXT STEP

Think hard: What do you have six of, but only six? If you have nothing, make it up and then write a mini-anecdote as to why you only have six.

Testing 1-2-3

1 **CHOOSE ONE WORD THAT MOST APPEALS TO YOU:**

trophy	giraffe	crush	mask
bible	weed	banana	gas
inhale	lava	fender	diaper

2 **CHOOSE ONE SETTING THAT MOST APPEALS TO YOU:**

at a circus	under a full moon
during a war	on a beach
in a space station	at a park

3 **CHOOSE ONE STARTING PHRASE THAT MOST APPEALS TO YOU:**

If I could stop ...

I once asked ...

The first day ...

If you must know ...

The hurricane neared ...

Start your story with this phrase, and incorporate the setting and word you chose.

TAKE THE NEXT STEP

Many things come in threes, including three-word expressions like "live, love, laugh" and "hip, hip, hooray." List all that come to mind. Set a timer for ten minutes, and include all the phrases in a story. Ready, set, go!

SPIN THE BOTTLE

Finish the story. Start with: *At my first boy-girl party I ...*

TAKE THE NEXT STEP

Give titles to your current life as if it was a ...

- teen movie:________________________________
- romance novel:________________________________
- sitcom:________________________________
- country song:________________________________
- mystery novel:________________________________
- home and garden show:________________________________

One Day at a Time

Time to write a story in bits and pieces. Hereafter, whenever you pick up this book, come back to this page. Today, begin with the given starter and write until you get to the first dot. Tomorrow, write until you get to the second dot ... and so on. (There are sixteen dots.)

I remember that hairstyle ...

TAKE THE NEXT STEP

Not many people like their driver's license or school photos. Create a character sketch of someone who does.

TAKE A SEAT

Write the story. Start with: *His chair ...*

TAKE THE NEXT STEP

When you sit up in your chair, use good posture, hold your pen properly, and originate slow breaths from your diaphragm (below your rib cage), you are able to think (and write) more clearly and evenly. To feel the difference, copy a sentence or two from this page while employing good posture. Doing so lends itself to optimal writing.

Van Go

Use the following two items in a story: Van Gogh and Van Go. Set the story in the year 2121. And start with: *The swirl of colors ...*

TAKE THE NEXT STEP

When you wash your van or car, do you wash some, then wax some, and then repeat? Or do you wash all and then wax all? In terms of writing and editing, it's best to write all and then edit all. Doing so keeps your right brain and left brain separate but equal. You've completed this page—now go back and edit it. Make it shine like a newly waxed convertible.

Peephole 2

You look through the peephole of your front door and see a face. Play out the story. Start with: *Sometimes I wish I came from a small family ...*

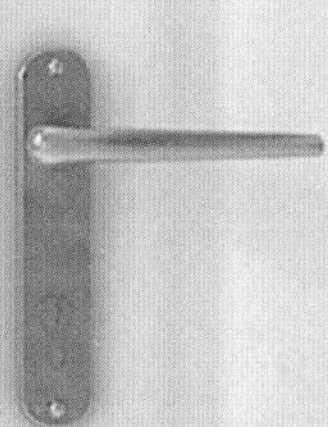

TAKE THE NEXT STEP

We can't choose our family, but we can choose our friends. Trace your connections until you link yourself to a famous writer (like in the game "Six Degrees of Kevin Bacon").

Once upon a Time

Ah—the classic opener, but with a twist! Pick one of these anagrams of "Once upon a Time" to add to the starter to make your story a lot more interesting:

Tame Puce Onion	**Patio Cone Menu**	**Nine Moo Teacup**	**Uneaten Pic Moo**	**Open Out Cinema**
Matinee Coupon	**Cootie Name Pun**	**Pee Icon Amount**	**Atom Pine Ounce**	**Canine Mope Out**
Oat Cup Nominee	**Taco Ennui Poem**	**No Manic Toupee**	**Cameo Peon Unit**	**Minute Ocean Op**
Aunt Moon Piece	**Open Me Auction**	**Em Union Toecap**	**Mention a Coupe**	**Petunia Come On**

Finish the story. Start with: *Once upon a time, long before the* ____________________ ...
(fill in the anagram here)

TAKE THE NEXT STEP

List six memories from the Februarys (or the FURY BEARS, SAFER RUBY, FURRY BASE, RUB FRY SEA, SURF YE BRA) of your life. Use these to prompt further writings.

CONTAGIOUS

Fill in the blanks with the first word that comes to mind:

A piece of furniture: ________________________________

A food product: ________________________________

A word about religion: ________________________________

A type of shoe: ________________________________

A sports verb: ________________________________

A body part: ________________________________

Use these six words in your story. Start with: *I remember catching ...*

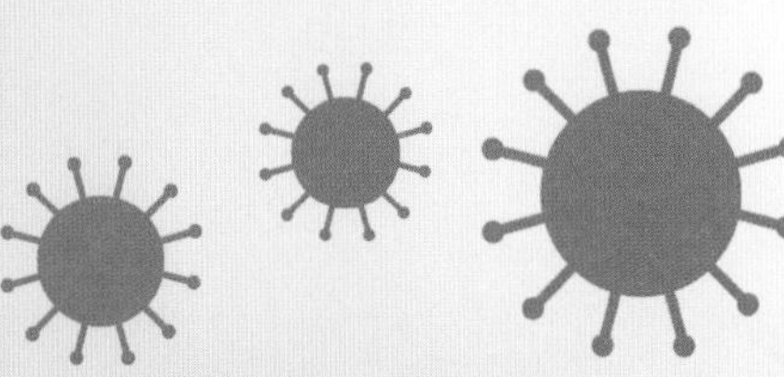

TAKE THE NEXT STEP

The word *should* is contagious. Before you know it, you are *should*-ing all over yourself. List the top three creativity-related tasks you think you *should* be doing, and replace *should* with *want*.

1. I want to ... ________________________.
2. I want to ... ________________________.
3. I want to ... ________________________.

Do something to satisfy each of these wants.

Tilt-A-Whirl

One way to create new nerve pathways in your brain is to modify how you do basic and familiar tasks. The term for it is *neurobics*, and some classic examples are brushing your teeth or dialing the phone with your opposite hand. You can give your brain an extra workout while writing by tilting your paper in the opposite direction from how you normally tilt it.

Most right-handers tilt their paper this way:  and lefties tilt it like this: 

Today try tilting your paper the opposite way—as extreme as you can without straining your wrist. If you typically keep your paper straight, pick the more uncomfortable tilted position. Write until you get to the end of the page. Start with: *The Tilt-A-Whirl operator ...*

TAKE THE NEXT STEP

Amusement park rides like the Tilt-A-Whirl are exhilarating for some and terrifying for others. The same holds true for various facets of writing. I feel exhilarated when I get to read my writing aloud. Others feel terror (or dread at best). What area(s) cause you the most excitement?

Focus on these. Do not let the areas that invoke terror stop you from being creative. When the time is right, you will figure out ways to tilt the terror on its head and make it through.

IF IT AIN'T BROKE

Finish the story. Start with: *It's not like it hasn't been broken before ...*

TAKE THE NEXT STEP

What does your creative writing cycle look like? Wavy lines, an uphill diagonal surge, scattered broken lines, etc.? Draw a map to depict it. Add next week's practice now to see if you can project its trajectory.

CHERRY

CHERRY

Think about a cherry ... the feel, smell, taste, color. While in this "sensing" frame of mind, write using this starter: *Her cheeriness makes me ...*

TAKE THE NEXT STEP

Which of your senses do you use most often in your writing? Which do you use least? Go back and add this sense to the story on this page. (Add it twice!) Remember to use it in your future writings as well.

FALL BACK

Finish the story. Start with: *Sometimes it's best not to have a safety net to fall back on ...*

TAKE THE NEXT STEP

Trace back through your entire life, listing all the stepping-stone episodes that led to this writing exercise in this book today. Pretty cool, huh?

SPRING FORWARD

Finish the story. Start with: *Sometimes you just have to take a leap of faith ...*

TAKE THE NEXT STEP

Sending your writing out into the world requires taking a leap of faith. Write about what your life will be like if you *don't* take the leap and send out your writing. Time to take the leap!

Walk in the Park

ONE • You are out walking. Two joggers pass you. You overhear a tidbit of their conversation: "... And the explosion was so ..." You are certain this is what you heard. Imagine on paper what it is they were talking about (or continue their conversation in dialogue format).

TAKE THE NEXT STEP

There's no such thing as an overnight success. You're on a talk show now and have been asked to describe the major events that led up to when you exploded onto the writing scene. Use lots of details.

TWO • You are out jogging. When two casual walkers dressed impeccably in old-fashioned garb pass you, you overhear a tidbit of their conversation: "When we meet Mr. Franklin at Carpenter Hall, I beseech you address him by his full surname and not merely call him Benjamin ... " You are certain this is what you heard. Imagine on paper what they were talking about (or continue their conversation in dialogue format).

TAKE THE NEXT STEP

With minimal formal education, Ben Franklin taught himself to write by copying and recopying the writings of others. One of his famous sayings is "Tell me, and I forget. Teach me, and I may remember. Involve me, and I learn." Now that you have established a writing practice, how might you use this quote to help others get started?

Double or Nothing

Write using the starter. Whatever word you write on the first double line, you must use every time you come to another double line on the rest of the page. Start with: *He said, "Double or nothing?" And I answered ...*

TAKE THE NEXT STEP

I dare you to double your productivity right now and do another page or two—or three or four!—in this book.

SLANGUAGE of SLOVE

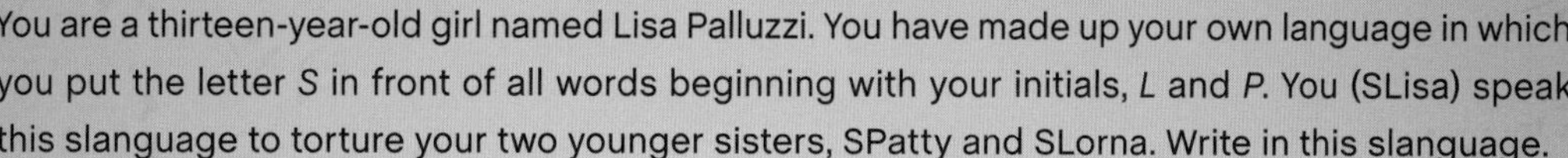

You are a thirteen-year-old girl named Lisa Palluzzi. You have made up your own language in which you put the letter *S* in front of all words beginning with your initials, *L* and *P*. You (SLisa) speak this slanguage to torture your two younger sisters, SPatty and SLorna. Write in this slanguage.

Start with: *When I babysit for you spipsqueaks on Saturday night, I am going to ...*

TAKE THE NEXT STEP

Who are you when it comes to your writing practice?

1. An underpaid teenage babysitter
2. A nanny from Europe
3. A retiree earning supplemental income
4. A well-behaved child
5. A poorly behaved child
6. Parents who are away

To be more productive, gain rewards, and still take care of yourself, who else might you be?

BUBBLE RAP-ONE

Create a dialogue between two people, using the speech bubbles provided. The bubbles are facing in two different directions, one for each person. There is a starter to get you on your way.

Come here often?

TAKE THE NEXT STEP

Imagine this shape is you:

And this shape is your writing practice:

Draw a representation of how they combine in your life. Examples:   

Card Tricks

Use all of the following in a story: **Queen of Hearts** • **Full Deck** • **Joker** • **Deal**
Start with: *I can't believe how easily I was tricked into ...*

TAKE THE NEXT STEP

Use your computer to make up business cards that detail your contact info as a writer. You'll look and feel professional, and you'll be taken more seriously when you network and make connections.

building BLOCKS

Use these six items like blocks, and build a story.

A man's first name

Another man's first name

A last name

An age

The name of a body of water

A setting

Start with: *The last time I ...*

TAKE THE NEXT STEP

List four ways you can build more writing time into your life. Perhaps you'll get up ten minutes earlier or write in line at the supermarket. Get out your calendar and start scheduling!

XMAS ON MARS

Write six words or phrases pertaining to Christmas here:

Start with: *Back when I was six and Mars was ...*

TAKE THE NEXT STEP

You may not get to go on a mission to Mars, but you can create a personal writing mission statement. Write one. (Cover principles, plans, who you are, foundations, etc.) Use it when you tell others about your writing.

ADVENTUROUS Adverbs

Use the adverbs as you get to them. Start with: *We left from ...*

madly

happily

insanely

mystically

desperately

TAKE THE NEXT STEP

Continue the adventure: Select one sentence from this story, and use it as a starter for another writing. To up the ante, this time use all ten of these adverbs in the new story: *unfortunately, adamantly, stealthily, methodically, furiously, erratically, mysteriously, stingingly, virtually, belatedly.*

TRISKAIDEKAPHOBIA 13

Use these thirteen words in your story:
book author mystery money success romance
wealth mansion play sci-fi star commitment bestseller

Start with: *I am terribly afraid ...*

TAKE THE NEXT STEP

There are probably 13 million excuses not to maintain your writing practice. When did you learn to make excuses for something you really want to do? Why do you still do it?

HAPPY ENDINGS • ONE

Use the last sentences at the bottom of the page to conclude your story.

... He left, and Mike pushed back his halo and got to work. He could see a lot of changes he wanted to make—

(The last two sentences are from *Stranger in a Strange Land* by Robert A. Heinlein.)

TAKE THE NEXT STEP

What excites you about ending a project? What scares you about ending a project? List ideas on how you can turn this fear into excitement every time.

PickyPicky

Finish the story. Start with: *The pickpocket gingerly ...*

TAKE THE NEXT STEP

From among all the possibilities, pick one goal you'd like to work towards in your writing tomorrow. First thing in the morning, do it. You'll feel great all day.

YOU MAY HAVE Already WON

You have received a believable-looking, business-sized white envelope in the mail. The return address is from a company called Peerless. Printed on the envelope in bright-red letters are the words "You May Have Already Won." Tell the story of what you may have won—or what you didn't win. Tell what you do with this envelope.

Start with: *Life takes some funny twists and turns ...*

TAKE THE NEXT STEP

You've just arrived at a two-week writing retreat that you won in a contest. Write a note home listing all you plan to accomplish.

Now do one (or all) of these things, whether you are at a retreat or sitting at your kitchen table.

BACK IN TIME

Write about a major event in your childhood. Write in first person as if you are, once again, that age and it just happened. Use child-appropriate language. Don't worry if the account turns out to be more fiction than fact. Start with: *Yesterday was ...*

Now write about the same event but as an adult looking back. Don't worry if the story changes this time; just go with the flow. Start with: *If I could go back in time to the day when ...*

TAKE THE NEXT STEP

List six memories from various Januarys in your life. Use these to prompt future writings.

Emoti-Cans AND Can'ts

Look at the ten emoticons on this page. To the side of each one, write the situation that prompted the expression. For example, Number 1 might be: Just ruined the surprise for a surprise birthday party. Number 2 could be: Going as one of the Blues Brothers for Halloween.

1.

2.

3.

4.

5.

6.

7.

8.

9.

10.

Pick a face/scenario combo that resonates with you. You are this person behind the face in this situation. Write starting with: *I can't...*

TAKE THE NEXT STEP

Although it's not universally accepted, many people believe that the subconscious mind does not understand negatives. Hypnotists take the safe route and always speak in positives. When it comes to self-talk, especially about your writing and writing talent, it's also best to err on the side of caution. Be an EMOTI-CAN and talk positively to yourself by using words like *can*, not *can't*.

GRAY MATTER

Finish the story. Start with: *It's the gray areas that ...*

TAKE THE NEXT STEP

If there was a writing scholarship in your honor, what would it be called? Who would be eligible? How often would it be given out? What would the criteria be? When and where would it be given? Would you be anonymous?

Sing Along

Song parodies are fun to write. All you have to do is sing the song in your head and replace the lyrics. You don't need to be able to carry a tune (I'm tone deaf). This is a great exercise if you're stuck in the car without a pen or paper. Find an oldies station and, as you listen to the songs, invent new lyrics.

Pick a number between 1 and 5 and locate it to the right. These are the lyrics to short children's songs for you to parody/rewrite. Think of a topic, and change the song's words to reflect this subject, paying attention to syllables and rhyme. When you're done, share it.

1\. "The Itsy-Bitsy Spider": The itsy-bitsy spider / Climbed up the waterspout / Down came the rain / And washed the spider out / Out came the sun / And dried up all the rain / And the itsy-bitsy spider / Climbed up the spout again.

2\. "Twinkle, Twinkle Little Star": Twinkle, twinkle, little star / How I wonder what you are! / Up above the world so high / Like a diamond in the sky / Twinkle, twinkle, little star / How I wonder what you are.

3\. "The Hokey Pokey": You put your right foot in / You put your right foot out / You put your right foot in and you shake it all about / You do the Hokey Pokey and you turn yourself around / That's what it's all about.

4\. "My Bonnie": My Bonnie lies over the ocean / My Bonnie lies over the sea / My Bonnie lies over the ocean / So bring back my Bonnie to me / Bring back, bring back / Oh bring back my Bonnie to me, to me / Bring back, bring back / Oh bring back my Bonnie to me.

5\. "Three Blind Mice": Three blind mice, three blind mice / See how they run, see how they run / They all ran after the farmer's wife / She cut off their tails with a carving knife / Did you ever see such a sight in your life / As three blind mice.

TAKE THE NEXT STEP

There are many people, pets, works of art, places in nature, stores, pens, computers, and so on that contribute to your current writing success. Don't let the word *success* scare you off, because, by doing this exercise, you are in the midst of experiencing a success. Take a moment now and write a paragraph of acknowledgments, singing the praises of all these people, places, and things that have helped you along the way. If you don't, they will remain unsung heroes. You don't want that to happen, do you?

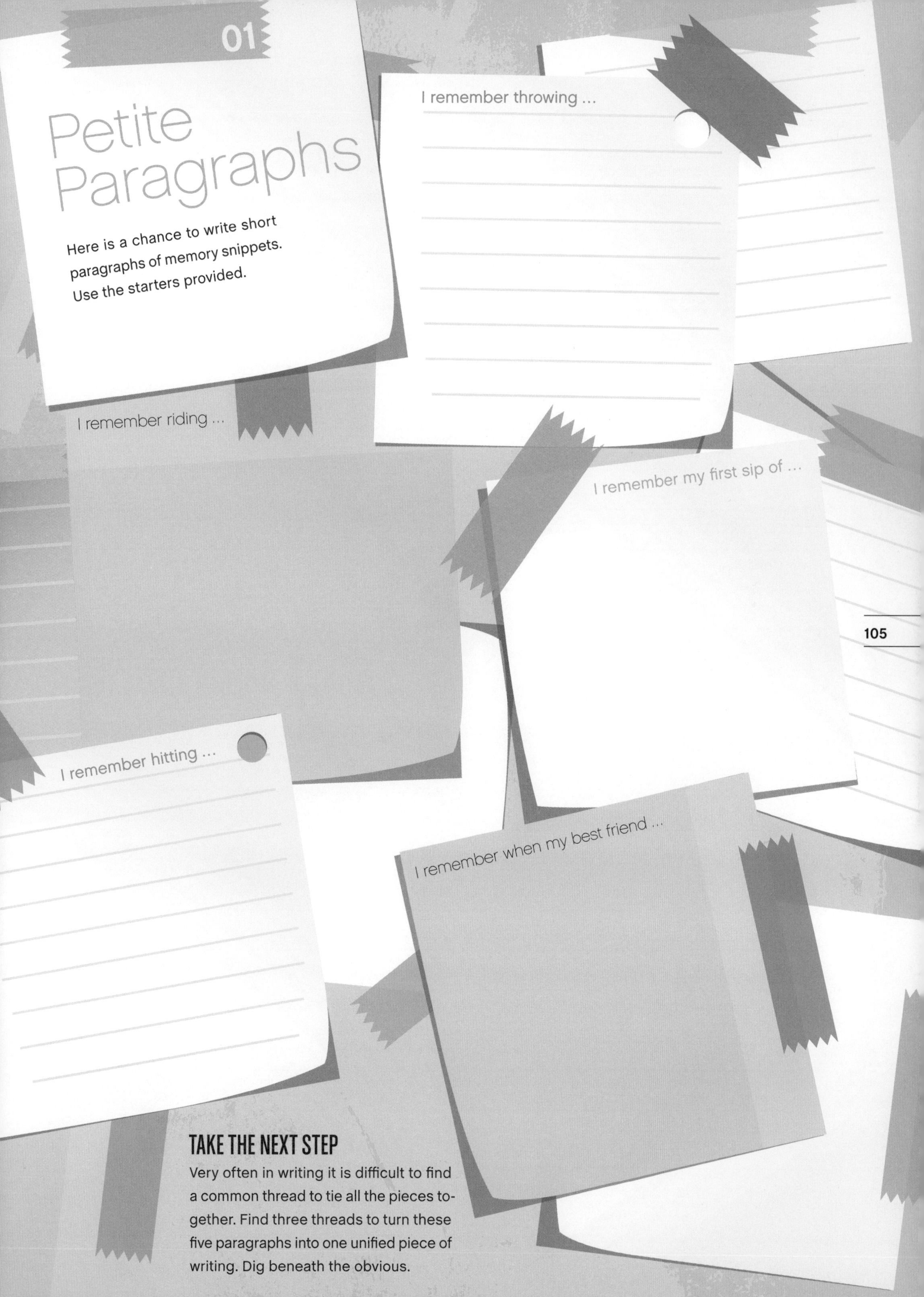

Petite Paragraphs

Here is a chance to write short paragraphs of memory snippets. Use the starters provided.

I remember throwing ...

I remember riding ...

I remember my first sip of ...

I remember hitting ...

I remember when my best friend ...

TAKE THE NEXT STEP

Very often in writing it is difficult to find a common thread to tie all the pieces together. Find three threads to turn these five paragraphs into one unified piece of writing. Dig beneath the obvious.

I, I, SIR

Whenever you get to the letter *I*, use it.
Start with: *The aisle was ...*

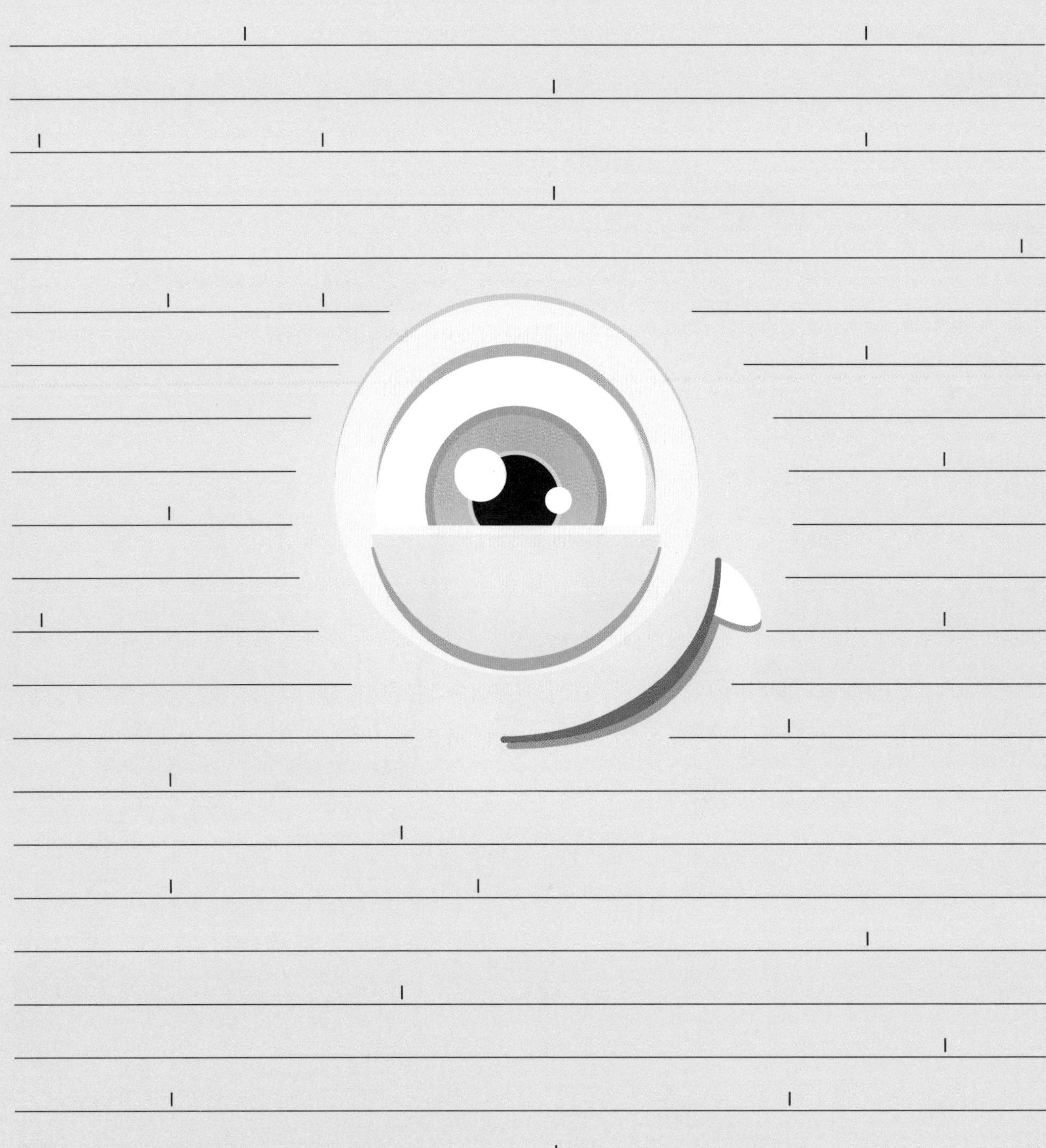

TAKE THE NEXT STEP

Write about yourself. Instead of using first person (*I*), use second person (*you*).

Idioms DELIGHT One

Start with the idiom *I don't usually hit the ground running ...*

In your conclusion, use the idiomatic expression *That's the way the cookie crumbles.*

TAKE THE NEXT STEP

If you approached your writing as if you were a pastry chef, what would you do differently? Try doing it the next time you write. See if your writing is different.

The classic assignment! Start with the given letter, and fill in each line with something you have done on various summer vacations. Focus on one year or many years. Example: *Ate overripe plums that dripped down my arms while I drove through Amish farm country.* The odder and stranger the entries, the better!

A ______

B ______

C ______

D ______

E ______

F ______

G ______

H ______

I ______

J ______

K ______

L ______

M ______

N ______

O ______

P ______

Q ______

R ______

S ______

T ______

U ______

V ______

W ______

X ______

Y ______

Z ______

TAKE THE NEXT STEP

Just like a photographer who shoots twenty-six pictures, the twenty-six items you wrote above are not equal in quality. "Summer better than others!" Go back through your writing and pick the one item that's the best shot in the roll. Circle it. Why did you pick this one?

Spoiled Rotten

List six disgusting things you've found in your refrigerator (or have heard others describe they've found in theirs):

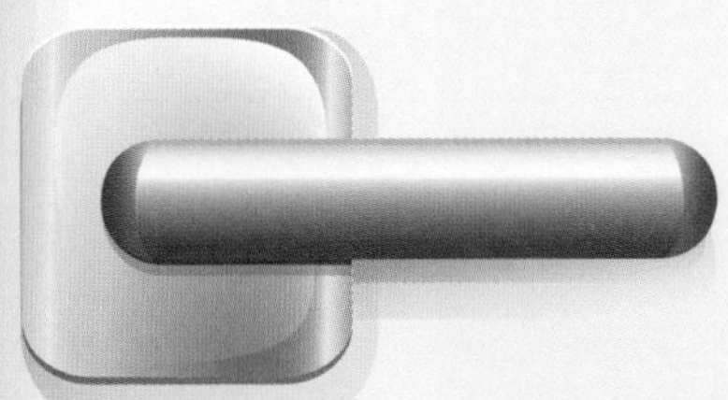

Use all six in a story. Start with: *Whenever he mentions Paris ...*

TAKE THE NEXT STEP

Many wonderful ideas come while doing mundane tasks. Have paper and a pencil handy to record ideas that come to you while you're washing dishes or driving long-distance. (Pull over to write, please!)

Grab that paper and pencil now so you don't miss out on a single creative writing idea!

SCARED STIFF

Finish the story. Start with: *He had a scar ...*

TAKE THE NEXT STEP

We all have emotional scars that keep us from writing what we want to write. Describe one of your scars as if it were a physical scar that you can actually see. Personify it. Did anything change for you?

Use all of these words. DIG**EST** • N**EST** • PROT**EST** • P**EST**

Start with: *Back in the sixties, or maybe it was already the seventies by then ...*

TAKE THE NEXT STEP

Here's a TEST for you. With ZEST, go back through this page of writing and figure out the BEST place to really start the story. Then number your sentences or paragraphs to reorder the REST of the tale. LEST you leave anything that is superfluous, cross out all that is not vital or necessary to the story. I can be a real PEST, can't I?

MARCH MUMBLE

Use the speech sounds as you get to them. Start with: *We marched ...*

oooh

shhhhh

TAKE THE NEXT STEP

Turn the radio dial to a music station you don't usually listen to. Listen until a song ends. How is what you just wrote similar to the song you heard? How is it different?

Exposing yourself to new things helps your writing grow.

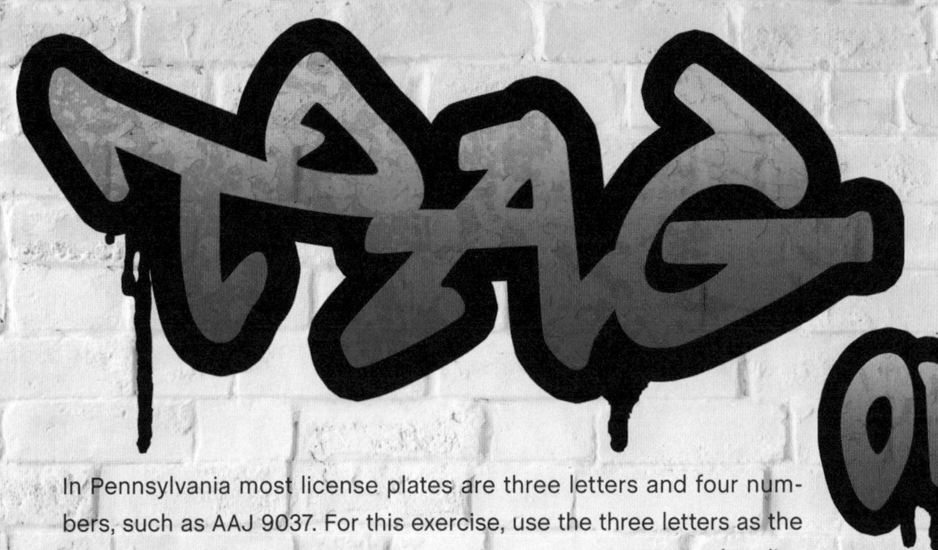

In Pennsylvania most license plates are three letters and four numbers, such as AAJ 9037. For this exercise, use the three letters as the first letters of the three beginning words in your story. Example: *Alice always joked ...* . Use the four-digit number, 9037, somewhere in your story.

Start here: A___________________ A___________________ J___________________...

TAKE THE NEXT STEP

You are about to start a game of writing-practice tag. You are "it" first, so you must immediately fill two pages with writing. Once you're done, tag a writer friend to be "it." Hand her two blank sheets of paper, and explain the simple rule of writing two pages before tagging someone else to be "it." Keep the game going!

OBJECTS NOT OF DESIRE

Use all these household objects in this story:

carrot peeler

toaster

floor lamp

toilet bowl brush

dish drainer

Start with: *The long ...*

TAKE THE NEXT STEP

What's the next step in your creative process? Are you resisting it? Don't you truly desire the end result? Or is it something else? What's the worst thing that will happen if you do it? Are you willing to take that risk?

STARING CONTEST

For this exercise, stare straight ahead. Don't look down at the page. Focus your eyes on an object and keep them there. Don't worry about your handwriting or neatness. Just enjoy the trance-like experience. Start with: *I see ...*

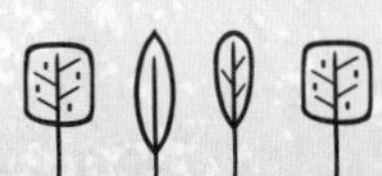

TAKE THE NEXT STEP

List what frightens or intimidates you about a blank page.

Do you realize it's possible you made up all those fears?

Now write what excites you about a blank page.

Feels better, doesn't it?

IT WAS A DARK AND STORMY NIGHT

The second most famous opener! Finish your story by using this line as the last seven words. Start with the most famous opener: *Once upon a time ...*

... it was a dark and stormy night.

TAKE THE NEXT STEP

Animals respond to danger with fight or flight. The same is true for writers. When things get challenging, do you fight by working harder or do you run away and abandon your writing? Write about when you stayed and worked something through to success.

Start with the word *apples* and write a story or poem, using each letter as you come to it.

APPLES ______ B ______

C ______ D ______

E ______ F ______

G ______ H ______

I ______ J ______

K ______ L ______

M ______ N ______

O ______ P ______

Q ______ R ______

S ______ T ______

U ______ V ______

W ______ X ______

Y ______ Z ______

TAKE THE NEXT STEP

Describe twenty-six of the infinite number of your positive writer-self traits, using each letter of the alphabet:

A______ B______ C______ D______ E______ F______ G______
H______ I______ J______ K______ L______ M______ N______
O______ P______ Q______ R______ S______ T______ U______
V______ W______ X______ Y______ Z______. Post this in your writing area.

Circle Game 2

Use all six words you circled in a story.
Start with: *I was completely captivated, like a ...*

CIRCLE TWO WORDS THAT APPEAL TO YOU:

peep
quest
rotten
sunshine
tarantula
undulate

CIRCLE TWO WORDS THAT APPEAL TO YOU:

viola
web
xylophone
zipper
astronaut
barracuda

CIRCLE TWO WORDS THAT APPEAL TO YOU:

calliope
desert
elegant
finesse
German
hysterical

TAKE THE NEXT STEP

"An exclamation mark is like laughing at your own joke." —F. Scott Fitzgerald

Exclamations seem to force the reader to feel something. You have a captive audience—don't lose them with exclamation overuse. Show them, don't force them. Go back through this book and eliminate as many exclamations as you can. Now! (Oops.)

MONSTER MASH

Use the words as you get to them. Start with:

Monsters don't ...

MASH

BASH

DASH

GASH

LASH

RASH

TAKE THE NEXT STEP

"Don't think and then write it down. Think on paper." —Harry Kemelman

Here's a chance to not reHASH. Write exactly what comes to mind at this moment. Don't lift your pen from the paper for at least two minutes.

Dressing on the Side

I once visited a creative nonfiction college class on Dress-Up Day, in which students were asked to wear a formal outfit or costume and tell the class a story related to it. Listening to the stories that used clothing as a backdrop, I learned a lot about each storyteller.

Choose one of these types of clothing:

1. A costume
2. A pair of shoes or sneakers
3. A pair of boots
4. A jacket or coat
5. A T-shirt or other shirt
6. Pajamas
7. Underpants (or some other undergarment)
8. A bathing suit
9. A hat or cap
10. A ring or other jewelry

Search the closets of your memory to find an item of this clothing type. Using this item as a starting point, from its acquisition to what happened when you wore it, tell a story about a life event. It's fascinating to see how much a story prompted by a single article of clothing can reveal about you, the narrator of the story.

Start your story with: *This particular ...*

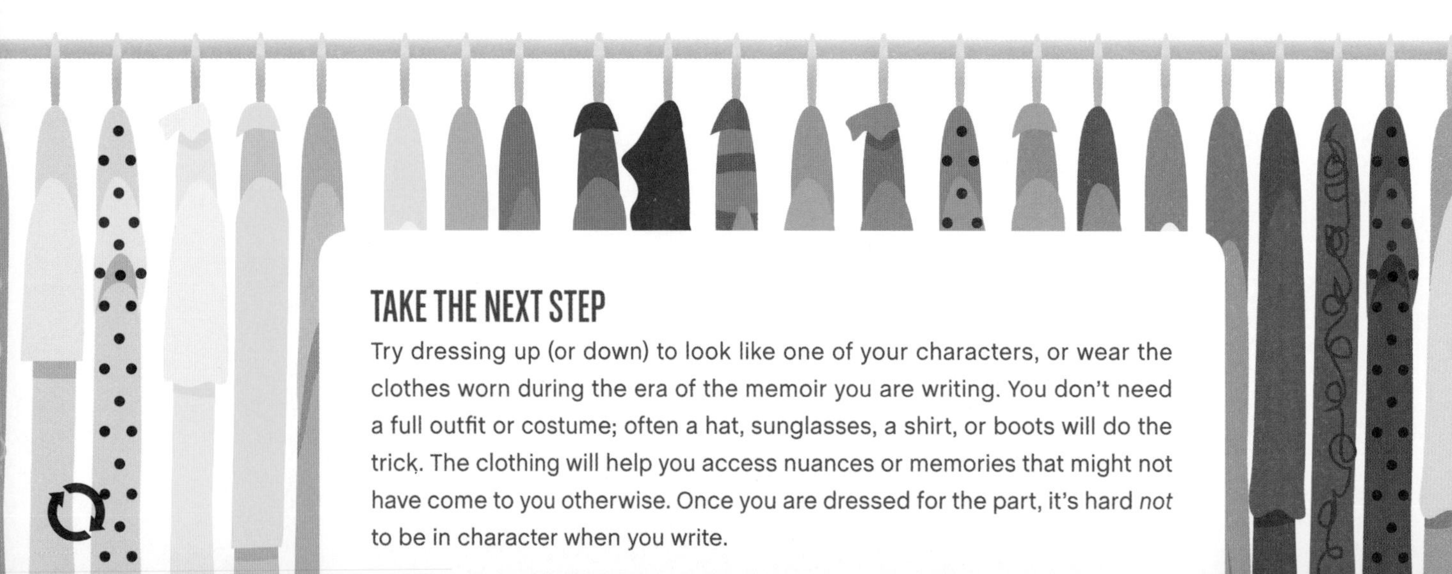

TAKE THE NEXT STEP

Try dressing up (or down) to look like one of your characters, or wear the clothes worn during the era of the memoir you are writing. You don't need a full outfit or costume; often a hat, sunglasses, a shirt, or boots will do the trick. The clothing will help you access nuances or memories that might not have come to you otherwise. Once you are dressed for the part, it's hard *not* to be in character when you write.

CURLEEEEEEECUE

If, while doing writing exercises, you go back and cross out a lot, hesitate while choosing a word, or write very methodically, you are probably allowing your left-brained editor to interfere with a right-brained activity. You can train yourself to keep a steady momentum so your left brain stays away until it's invited in.

To do this, start by training your hand, which will, in turn, train your brain.

Fill every line below with curlicues that look like cursive *E*s. If it's easier to do upside down *E*s, or undotted *I*s, that's fine. When done, your page should look like this:

TAKE THE NEXT STEP

Whenever you're unable to prevent your editor from stepping in while you're doing writing exercises, *stop immediately* and draw curlicues on a full sheet of paper as you did in this exercise. The action will get you back into right-brain mode where your pen moves swiftly across the page. When your hand and brain are better trained, you will need to do only one line of curlicues to get back in the right-brain, nonediting groove.

Now choose a starting phrase, and continue the story as you write directly over your lines of curlicues. Try to keep your pen moving at a quick speed as you did while drawing the curlicues. Resist going back and crossing out or inserting additional words. If you run out of ideas, draw curlicues until something new comes to mind. Write until every original curlicue is covered.

1. She dotted her *I*s with hearts ...
2. The writing on the wall of the cave ...
3. After his fifth-grade teacher told him he had the best handwriting ...
4. The detective was certain the handwriting was ...
5. While the weightlifter was doing a set of curls ...

Philly Phonetics

Whenever possible I like to put in a plug for my hometown, Philadelphia, Pennsylvania. Use these four linguistic gems from Philly in your story:

- *Youze* (more than one person in the second person, as in *Where youze goin'?*)
- *Mayan* (not yours, as in *Don't touch that, it's mayan!*)
- *Hoagie* (submarine sandwich, as in *Gimme a hoagie wit da works!*)
- *Down D' Shore* (New Jersey beach, as in *We left d'city early t'head down d'shore.*)

Start with: *We got two cheesesteaks t' go and ...*

TAKE THE NEXT STEP

What foods from your area can you mention in your writing to add local flavor? Make a list for future reference.

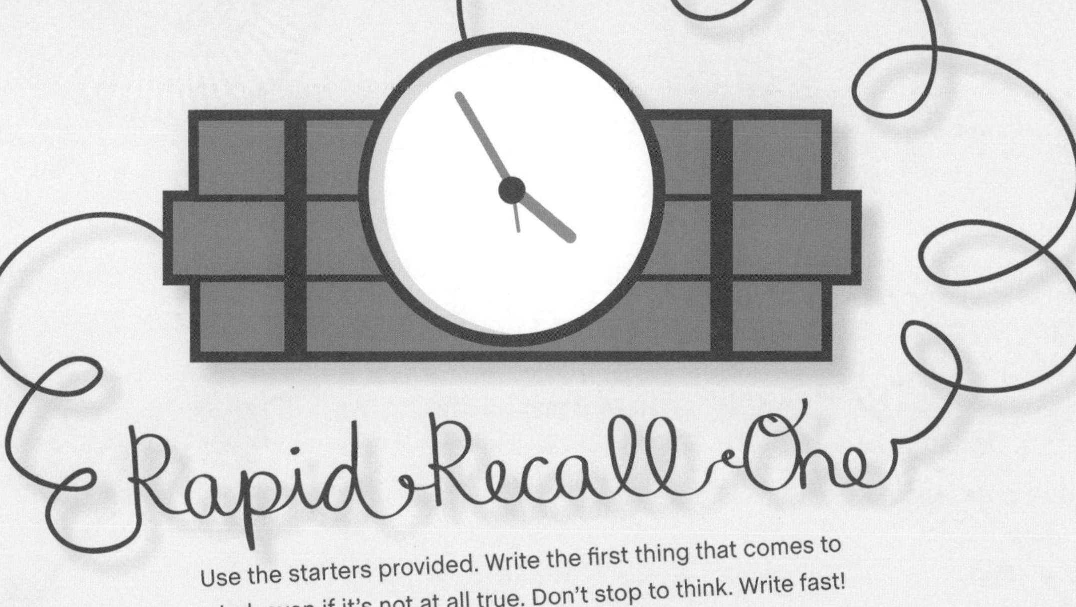

Use the starters provided. Write the first thing that comes to mind, even if it's not at all true. Don't stop to think. Write fast!

I RECALL A TIME WHEN …

THE PRODUCT RECALL …

I RECALL WRITING …

TAKE THE NEXT STEP

Recall six memories that happened during the months of March of your life. Use these to prompt further writings.

FRAMED

Use the shape as you choose.
A starter has been provided.

I was framed ...

TAKE THE NEXT STEP

Do you ever blame someone or something for where you are creatively? Do you ever give someone else credit when you have a creative success? Name the blame or credit source here: ___________________________

Now get a thick marker and cross out the name. You, and only you, are responsible for your creative successes and challenges.

CAMP PAIN · ONE

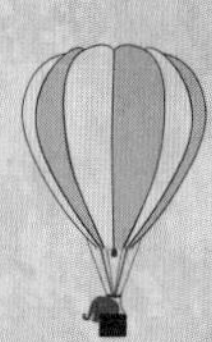

Write two words about fighting: ______________________________

Write two words about camping: ______________________________

Write two words about friendship: ______________________________

You are twelve years old and away at overnight camp. You just had a fight with your best friend. Write a letter home, incorporating the words you listed above.

Dear ____________________,

I'm never talking to ______________ ever again. Today ...

TAKE THE NEXT STEP

You can't always change a situation, but you can change who you are in the circumstance. Describe a current challenging situation. Describe who you might be (instead of your usual self) to make it better. Be this person tomorrow, and see what happens.

CAMP PAIN · TWO

Write two words about peace: ______________________________

Write two words about elections: ______________________________

Write two words about enemies: ______________________________

You are the best friend of the writer from the exercise above.
After your fight, you are also writing a letter home. Incorporate the six words from above.

Dear ____________________,

I don't want to hear the name ______________ ever again. Today ...

TAKE THE NEXT STEP

Many famous people have monikers by which they are known, such as "Grammar Girl, "Queen of Clean," and "The Boss." Come up with one to describe your writer-self.

Get in the right frame of mind by repeating your moniker aloud as you sit down to write.

Boy Band

You are the lead singer of a really hot, up-and-coming boy band. Your recently released single has been getting tons of play, and you are now on your first big tour as the opening act for a much more popular boy band. Your band is traveling together from city to city on a secondhand tour bus. Things have not been going as well as planned. Finish the story.

Although the girls scream and shout ...

TAKE THE NEXT STEP

Take note! Write a piece that is not about anything musical yet contains as many of these musical words as possible: *crescendo*, *beat*, *brass*, *cadence*, *chant*, *chorus*, *concert*, *flat*, *sharp*, *fiddle*, *serenade*, *prelude*, *percussion*, *octave*, *note*, *melody*, *minor*, *major*, *horn*, *voice*, *tempo*, *suite*, *harmony*, *staff*, *rhythm*, *wind*, *reed*, *sing*. Here's a starting phrase if you need one: *The dynamic duo ...*

SMELL A RAT

Write three smells you love:

Write three smells you hate:

Use all six scents in a piece starting with: *I pulled into the gas station ...*

TAKE THE NEXT STEP

When we were kids, my sister Hope loved the smell of gasoline. List quirks of others to add dimension to future characters.

Create an entire dialogue between two people who are texting. Each color phone screen represents one of the people. Write back and forth using the colors as shown. In some instances, one person will be sending multiple texts before the other responds.

Choose one of these scenarios:

- an apology
- an awkward invitation
- an accusation
- an announcement

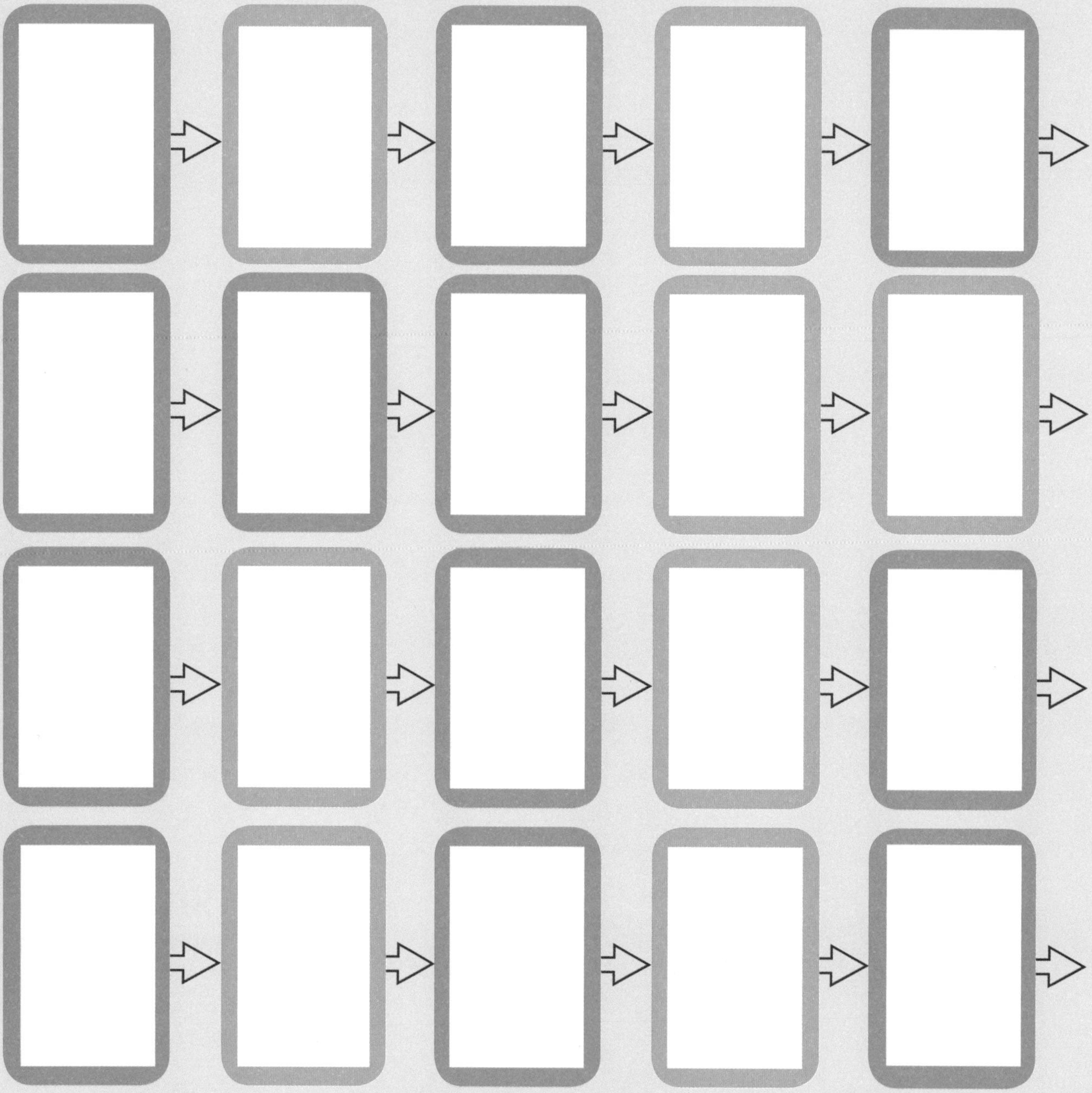

TK TH NXT STP

Creative inspiration often happens between two people who don't know each other and have never met. For example, one of the best ways to spark your own creativity is to participate in another's creations. This happens all the time when you watch movies, read books, and visit museums. Letting the passions of other creative people wash over you is a great way to become inspired. And when you share your work with the world, you are also paying forward the inspiration.

CRITIC'S CORNER

Answer the questions that appear in the shapes. Write (or draw) inside the shapes.

What does your inner critic smell like?

What do you say or do to make your inner critic quiet down or go away?

What does your inner critic sound like?

What does your inner critic look like?

What are some of your inner critic's favorite words?

How does your inner critic walk?

How does your inner critic frown?

TAKE THE NEXT STEP

Where would you like to send your critic? Photocopy this completed page, put it in an envelope, affix proper postage, and address it. Then mail it, sending your critic away. Afterward, throw yourself a little party and invite your muse!

Dreamy

Use the cloud shapes as you like. A starter is provided.

I remember dreaming ...

TAKE THE NEXT STEP

Don't cloud your writing by mumbling when you read it aloud. Stand tall and read what you've written out loud, enunciating every word. Read it over and over until you are certain that listeners will hear the pride you take in your creativity. Now do the same with a polished piece of writing. If you don't have one, find one to edit and then read it aloud with pride.

SHAKES-PEER

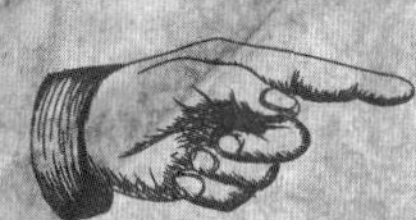

Use all these words that were coined by the Bard:

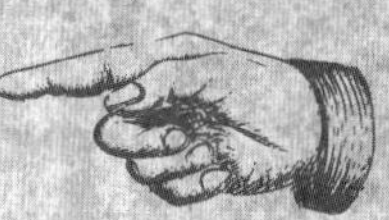

COLD-HEARTED • LUSTROUS
SAVAGERY • SWAGGER • WATCHDOG

Start with: ***Even though seeing him makes me shake, I still consider him my peer . . .***

TAKE THE NEXT STEP

Who in your life could be a role model for your writing practice? Think out of the box—it doesn't have to be a writer. Spend more time with him or her. For whom could your writing practice be a role model? Contact him or her, and spend time together.

GREEK GODS

Use the name of the Greek god as you get to each one on the page.

Start with: *Winning is not ...*

Ares

Zeus

Poseidon

Apollo

Eros

TAKE THE NEXT STEP

How are you at receiving praise? Do you blush? Smile? Hide? Look away? Deny it? It feels great to be able to take in every word. To practice, stare at yourself in a mirror. Make good eye contact, breathe slowly, touch your heart with one hand, and praise yourself. Do it until you feel comfortable hearing wonderful things about yourself.

Knot Now

Finish the story. Start with:
She adjusted his bow tie ...

TAKE THE NEXT STEP

Sometimes we need to be reminded to speak positively about ourselves. In terms of your writing, finish these sentences positively:

- I am ____________________. • I am ____________________.
- I am ____________________. • I am ____________________.

The next time you're asked if you are a writer, don't hem and haw or make excuses. Simply say, "I am."

TERRIBLE TWOS

You are two years old. Fill in the following prompts from this perspective.
Be childlike! *Play!*

Give yourself a name with the initials C.A.T.: ______

Nickname: ______

Eye color: ______

Hair color: ______

Favorite food: ______

Siblings' names and ages: ______

How your siblings treat you: ______

Thoughts on toilet training: ______

Start with: *Here I am, stuck in my crib ...*

TAKE THE NEXT STEP

In what area of your creativity are you stuck?

A new adhesive remover has been invented, guaranteed to get you unstuck. What's the first creative step you'll take now that you're free?

I FAILED JAIL

Use the words as you come to them. Start with: *When I opened my eyes and realized I was in jail ...*

JAIL

FAIL BAIL

HAIL MAIL

NAIL PAIL

RAIL

SAIL

TAIL

FAIL

JAIL

TAKE THE NEXT STEP

Is there an issue or a person for whom you'd go to jail? Who? What? Why? If you fuel your writing with this type of emotion, it will always be powerful to the reader.

HAPPY ENDINGS 2

Use the last sentence at the bottom of the page to conclude your story.

Again he paced the floor, but his path was not nine feet by two. (The last sentence is from *Ann Vickers* by Sinclair Lewis.)

TAKE THE NEXT STEP

Pacing yourself when writing a long piece is very helpful. Describe how you can use goals, a timer, rewards, or other tools to keep your writing on time and on target. Perhaps you are already using these tools in other facets of your life.

DO YOU HAIKU?

Your assignment is
To write a haiku today.
Help is on this page.

Haiku are Japanese poems composed of seventeen syllables in three lines: The top line has five syllables, the middle line has seven syllables, and the bottom line has five syllables. The assignment above is actually a haiku. The "help" to which it refers is the plethora of five-syllable lines listed on this page. Choose two you like (or pick two randomly), and write them at the bottom of the page on lines 1 and 3. Add your own seven-syllable middle line, and voilà, you've written a haiku.

A hidden treasure
A knife and a fork
Above the girl's head
Acting like a jerk
An unfolded map
Anger in his blood
Anonymously
Birds chirping at night
Blindingly bright sun
Broken promises
Burst water balloons
Cards on the table
Chinese take-out food
Cookie dough ice cream
Curiosity
Dancing in the dark
Dazzling harp music
Dealt quite a good hand
Downloading music
Drunk on happiness
Eyes to the future
Fell like dominoes
Field of red tulips
Five minutes of fame
Generational
Glittering gemstones
Halloween candy
Hard work rewarded

Heart stuck in the past
Homework assignment
Ice-skating at dusk
In a traffic jam
In muddy waters
In this dream of ours
Inebriated
Internet dating
Intoxicating
Is full of regret
Kissed by summer sun
Kites dancing on air
Last leaves of autumn
Laughing through the night
Let the race begin
Lighthearted laughter
Like an octopus
Like bitter honey
Little villages
Lost and later found
Magician's rabbit
Many sparkling lights
Milk and three cookies
Monday always comes
Money for nothing
Morning came quickly
Neighborly gestures
Oatmeal chocolate chip

On an old sailboat
On an island cruise
On the DVD
On the edge of time
Overachiever
Peanuts and a prize
Perched on a tree branch
Picnic in the park
Questioning children
Raised on rock and roll
Rewards never claimed
Robotic gestures
Roller coaster ride
Seagulls on the surf
Seen from the window
Shaded from the sun
Sharing cups of tea
Shouldering the load
Six-digit income
Smile for the camera
Soaring in the sky
Stores of hidden joy
Stories never shared
Strumming the guitar
Student of the earth
Sunny-side-up eggs
Swirling in the lake
Taking a first step

The means to an end
The morning paper
The sound of water
The summer river
The town is silent
Thick, flowing lava
Through the wooded park
Thunder struck the field
Time to eat my words
Tumbling down the hill
Two text messages
Tyrannosaurus
Umbrella in hand
Unanimously
Unconventional
Under hypnosis
Under the boardwalk
Unfortunately
Unopened presents
Unwritten stories
Voters stood in line
Who are the mothers
Winter turned to spring
With a writer's eyes
With queen-like posture
Worn piano keys
Written in pencil
Yes, no, or maybe

Write your haiku here:

1. ______________________

2. ______________________

3. ______________________

And if you're still feeling the call of seventeen syllables, write another one here:

1. ______________________

2. ______________________

3. ______________________

TAKE THE NEXT STEP

Twitter is the perfect place to share your haiku creations. I challenge you to entertain friends by writing and tweeting (in 140 characters or less) one haiku (seventeen syllables) a day for the next week (seven days). You've already started with the haikus above.

Stream of Consciousness

Start with the word *conscious* and free-associate. Write down whatever comes to mind. Example: *pillow, sleep, dream, flying, pink sky, aliens, music, Beethoven, rock ...*

CONSCIOUS

Circle eight interesting words and use them in a story. Start with: *The sparkling trout stream ...*

TAKE THE NEXT STEP

Free-associate again, starting with the word *commitment.*

Do these words reveal anything new to you about your writing self? Are there some positive ones you can circle? Or do you need to work on adding them?

Fill the page. Start with: *She found joy in the most ...*

TAKE THE NEXT STEP

"Fear is that little darkroom where negatives are developed." —Michael Pritchard

Where do you relish your creative joys? Be spontaneous and visit one of these places today. If you can't physically go, then venture there in your imagination.

NOVEMBERTH

FINISH THE STORY. Start with: *I found myself in the berth of the spaceship November ...*

TAKE THE NEXT STEP

Travel back mentally and list six memories from Novembers past. Use these to prompt further writings.

DISASTER AVERTED

USE THESE FOUR WORDS:
tickle • tear • target • locket

TAKE THE NEXT STEP

No need to give tomorrow's writing practice any chance for disaster. Write the ideal horoscope for yourself. Read it tomorrow before you write to make sure its predictions are sure to come true.

START WITH: *What a disaster ...*

MUSE-INGS

A chance to invite your muse for a visit! If you don't believe you have one, make one up. Answer the questions directly in the boxes—or even draw if you prefer.

What does your muse walk like?

What does your muse sound like?

What does your muse do for fun?

What does your muse wear?

How does your muse smile?

Where does your muse live?

What does your muse like to eat?

What does your muse smell like?

TAKE THE NEXT STEP

Write a thank-you note to your muse. Read it out loud so you can take in every word!

Use all of these spices in your story: **.: OREGANO :. .: WASABI :. .: GINGER :. .: GARLIC :. .: CILANTRO :. .: CINNAMON :.**

Start with: *On the surface, she was sweet as sugar, but underneath, she was ...*

TAKE THE NEXT STEP

Chefs know the best spices to use to tickle the tongue of the eater. Writers know the best words to use to inspire the imagination of the reader. Go back through this writing, and spice it up with the best possible adjectives you can conjure. Use a thesaurus if you like. Make it a delicious treat for the imagination.

take your places

To make a location such as a foreign place come alive in your writing, it's helpful to intersperse some easily understood words and phrases from that area. While doing your best to use these French words in your writing, try not to overwhelm your readers or make them feel like they need a dictionary.

Start with: *I took a sip ...*

ALLONS-Y: Let's go!

BAGUETTE: a long, narrow loaf of bread with a crisp crust

CRÈME FRAÎCHE: "fresh cream," a heavy cream slightly soured but not as sour or as thick as sour cream

ÉLAN: a distinctive flair or style

EN ROUTE: on the way

FAIT ACCOMPLI: something that has already happened and is thus unlikely to be reversed; a done deal

GENDARME: a policeman

JE NE SAIS QUOI: an indefinable "something" that distinguishes the object in question from others

JOIE DE VIVRE: joy of life/living

MADEMOISELLE: young unmarried lady, miss

MÉLANGE: a mixture

OBJET D'ART: a work of art, also a utilitarian object displayed for its aesthetic qualities

PAR AVION: by plane

POSEUR: a poser, a wannabe

RIVE GAUCHE: the left bank of the River Seine in Paris

SOIRÉE: an evening party.

VIN DE PAYS: "country wine"; wine of a lower designated quality

TAKE THE NEXT STEP

If you enjoyed this exercise, try it again with these German words: *stein, frankfurter, blitzkreig, angst, hinterland, autobahn, wunderkind, wurst, pumpernickel, karabiner, rucksack, dachshund, dreck, gesundheit, dummkopf, hausfrau, Volkswagen, lederhosen, verboten, kitsch.*

Use the starters provided and the shapes as you like.

TAKE THE NEXT STEP

If you have a new angle on an issue, write an op-ed piece and send it to your local media. If it's published, it's a good way to get a bit of local fame and can also be a stepping-stone to other writing opportunities. Jot down some op-ed ideas now.

This is a fave of mine 'cause it makes you dig for words. Each word in this piece must be one syllable.

Start with: *The bull ...*

TAKE THE NEXT STEP

In terms of creative writing, which step in the process brings out the stubborn bull in you? Getting started? Writing the middle? Finishing? Editing? Sending it into the world? Jot down some ideas to turn your stubborn bull into an easygoing lamb. Try one, and see if it helps.

TRAIT ME RIGHT

Before looking below, pick five numbers between 1 and 50 and write them here: ___________

Now locate your chosen numbers in this grid of traits and attributes. All five traits will combine to describe one character. Give this character a name: ___________

Blue eyes 1	Gregarious 2	Nervous 3	Tiny Mouth 4	Tall 5	Procrasti-nator 6	Impulsive 7	Couch Potato 8	Cat Person 9	Baby-Faced 10
Easily Blushes 11	Housebound 12	Phlegmy 13	Miserly 14	Limps 15	Overbite 16	Small Family 17	Mumbler 18	Flighty 19	Rough 20
Nine Toes 21	Snobby 22	Guilt-Ridden 23	Whimsical 24	In Debt 25	Runny Nose 26	Immature 27	Loud Laugh 28	Acne 29	Excitable 30
Intuitive 31	Jealous 32	Protective 33	Cunning 34	Phobic 35	Toothless 36	Noncon-forming 37	Night Owl 38	Compas-sionate 39	Petty 40
Forgetful 41	Inspiring 42	Freckled 43	Stubborn 44	Lonely 45	Groggy 46	Hardworking 47	Mensa Member 48	Obese 49	Thick-Skinned 50

Write a piece from the point of view of your character, incorporating his or her traits and attributes. Do not merely mention these traits; show them through dialogue, actions, and description.

Start with: *Of all the people in town ...*

TAKE THE NEXT STEP

Write a list of traits that a committed writer embodies. Circle all the ones you currently exhibit. Underline one that you would like to add to your repertoire. Now set a series of goals to make this trait one you can call your own. Once you embody it, come back and choose a new trait to add.

CHOICES, CHOICES

Choose one:

A. I'd like to be able to fly using my own powers.

B. I'd like to be able to make myself invisible.

You now possess this superpower for the story you are about to write. Start with: *It was just a teeny-weeny little lie ...*

TAKE THE NEXT STEP

Try this teeny-weeny exercise: Set a timer for ten minutes, get comfortable—but not too comfy—and think about writing. Do not write, do not take notes, and do not jot anything down—no matter how much you want to during the ten minutes. Just think about writing ...

What happened for you? Are you surprised?

TAG 2

In Pennsylvania, most license plates are three letters and four numbers, such as CAD 2322. For this exercise, use the three letters as the first letters of the three beginning words in your story. Example: *Come and donate ...* Use the four-digit number, 2322, somewhere in your story. Example: *Make your donations at Smiley Bank at 2322 Main Street.*

START HERE ...

C ______________ **A** ______________ **D** ______________

TAKE THE NEXT STEP

Playing tag was a carefree way to spend summer evenings. If there were no deadlines and no expectations, what would be your writing equivalent to playing tag?

Perhaps you've been playing all this time and didn't know it.

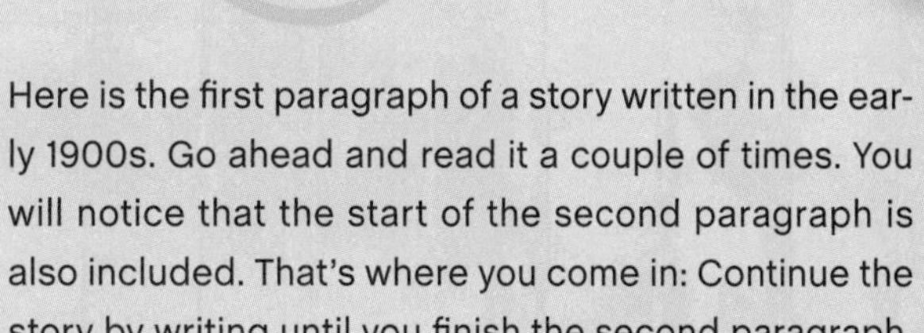

Here is the first paragraph of a story written in the early 1900s. Go ahead and read it a couple of times. You will notice that the start of the second paragraph is also included. That's where you come in: Continue the story by writing until you finish the second paragraph.

> The most merciful thing in the world, I think, is the inability of the human mind to correlate all its contents. We live on a placid island of ignorance in the midst of black seas of infinity, and it was not meant that we should voyage far. The sciences, each straining in its own direction, have hitherto harmed us little; but some day the piecing together of dissociated knowledge will open up such terrifying vistas of reality, and of our frightful position therein, that we shall either go mad from the revelation or flee from the deadly light into the peace and safety of a new dark age.

Theosophists have guessed at the ...

TAKE THE NEXT STEP

The paragraph to the left is taken from the story *The Call of Cthulhu* by H.P. Lovecraft. (The title of this exercise was a clue to the author's name.) As a special treat, there is no further assignment for you today. Instead, you get to read how the author continued the story:

> Theosophists have guessed at the awesome grandeur of the cosmic cycle wherein our world and human race form transient incidents. They have hinted at strange survivals in terms which would freeze the blood if not masked by a bland optimism. But it is not from them that there came the single glimpse of forbidden aeons which chills me when I think of it and maddens me when I dream of it. That glimpse, like all dread glimpses of truth, flashed out from an accidental piecing together of separated things—in this case an old newspaper item and the notes of a dead professor. I hope that no one else will accomplish this piecing out; certainly, if I live, I shall never knowingly supply a link in so hideous a chain. I think that the professor, too, intended to keep silent regarding the part he knew, and that he would have destroyed his notes had not sudden death seized him.

Use the image as you like.

Start with: *Leaving the seat up ...*

151

TAKE THE NEXT STEP

Get a big bowl, fill it with warm water, and soak your feet while writing.

Start with: *I am floating ...*

I'VE TOLD YOU A MILLION TIMES!

Write three action words (verbs):

Write three descriptive words (adjectives):

Use them all in a story. Start with: *If I've told you once, I've told you a million times ...*

TAKE THE NEXT STEP

There are a million ways to show characters' emotions. Practice writing scenes using these character and emotion combos:

- nurse/pride
- beautician/dread
- custodian/jealousy

MORAL ONE

Use the moral at the bottom of the page to conclude the story you are about to write.

Start with: *Back when I was ...*

And the moral of the story is: *The apple doesn't fall far from the tree.*

TAKE THE NEXT STEP

I promised myself that when I got a book deal I'd buy myself a fruit-of-the-month club. Whenever a catalog arrived I was reminded of my prize and my progress. What goal do you want to attain? What gift would you give yourself after you achieved it?

FINISH THE STORY. Start with: *Miss Understanding, the librarian, opened a can of worms by ...*

TAKE THE NEXT STEP

Readers understand more when you show instead of tell. Here's an example of telling: *My brother is funny and smart.* And here's an example of showing: *My brother had the crowd in stitches as he sang the periodic table a la Frank Sinatra.* Now turn the following "tell" into a "show": *He was tired and happy.*

THE GREAT DIVIDE

USE BOTH STARTERS.

He never stops to ask for directions ...

Even when we're not lost, she ...

TAKE THE NEXT STEP

If you were to divide your life in the last year into two parts, writing and not writing, what percent was spent writing? What percent was spent not writing?

Starting today and continuing for one full year, what percentage would you like to spend writing? Block out the time now—for the entire year!

FINISH ALL FOUR OF THESE SHORTS. The starter will stay constant, but your name will change.

Your name is Celeste. Start with: *He told me ...*

Your name is Bertha. Start with: *He told me ...*

Your name is Hank. Start with: *He told me ...*

Your name is Percy. Start with: *He told me ...*

TAKE THE NEXT STEP

Circle the name in this list that most appeals to you: Acel, Bewn, Copi, Dov, Ekna, Flyt, Gerf, Hasz, Itan, Julp, Karn, Loli, Meln, Nant, Ompa, Pury, Quij, Rolt, Sanu, Truf, Urat, Vran, Weqy, Xply, Yfra, Zigp. If this was your name, how might your writing be different? Tomorrow, write as if you are this person.

Solitaire, Anyone?

If you love word games, here's a chance to play one and, at the same time, get in a writing session. Your goal is to use as many words as possible in your piece that contain a certain pair of letters. Each time you write a word containing the letter pair, you get one point. Of course, there's a catch: You can only score a word once. If you're using the letter pair *US*, you score one point the first time you use the word *us* and no points every time thereafter. Word variations, like plurals and past tense, are considered new words the first time you use them. Proper nouns and acronyms also count, so *SUSan* and *USA* would net you one point each. Words that use the pair more than once earn an automatic ten points. Try for as many points as possible. Use the same letter pair again to try to beat your score.

Example (words with the letter pair *UR* that all score one point): *pURple, URgent, URgently, URology, URologist, occUR, occURs, occURred, occURring, URL, URuguay*

Pick a letter-pair.

1. OR
2. UP
3. AR
4. IR
5. UR
6. AP
7. EP
8. IP
9. OP
10. UD

Start with: *Like most lovers of ...*

TAKE THE NEXT STEP

Writing is often a very solitary experience, but it doesn't have to be. After I created this exercise, I sent it to a friend who posted it on her blog. I asked for guinea pigs to try it, hot off the press, and give feedback. Blogs, websites, Twitter, Facebook, Instagram, and so on are great platforms for inviting others into your creative process. Thanks to the Internet you have a worldwide pool of people with whom you can share ... and due to time differences, there's always someone awake and ready to give and get feedback.

PETITE PARAGRAPHS 2

Here is a chance to write short paragraphs of memory snippets. Use the starters provided.

I remember running ...

I remember spitting ...

I remember growing ...

I remember Valentine's Day ...

I remember liking ...

I remember feeling ...

TAKE THE NEXT STEP

Take one phrase from each of these six paragraphs and combine them to form a six-line poem. Cool, huh?

SILENT TREATMENT

Finish the story. Start with: *We sat in silence for ...*

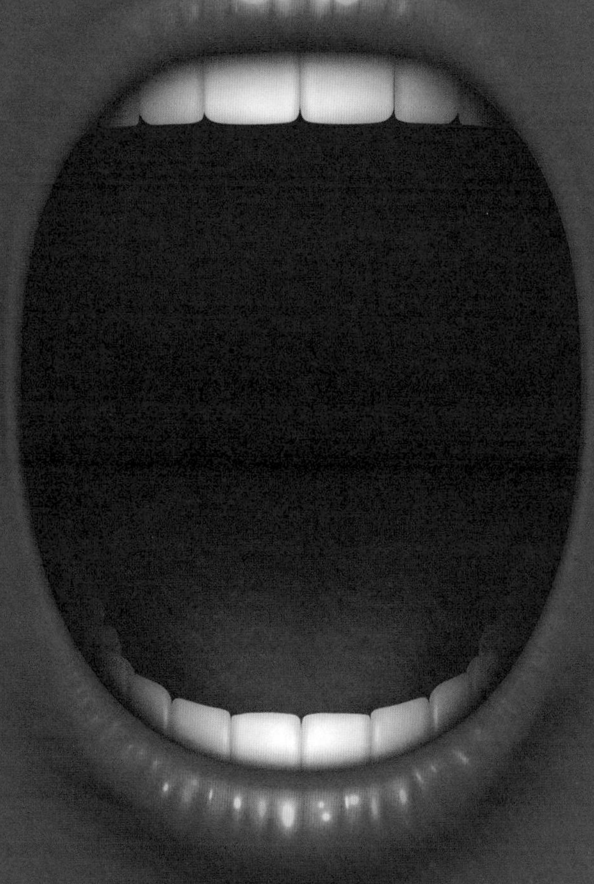

TAKE THE NEXT STEP

Very often when someone critiques us, we remain silent (intentionally or unintentionally). Here's a chance to tell off one of those critiquers. Grab a pen and paper, and go to town!

gotta lotta

When Louis Armstrong was asked what jazz is, he replied, "Man, if you gotta ask, you'll never know." Use this quote in a story. There's no need to reference jazz or Louis Armstrong unless you want to.

Start with: *The captain shouted, "Anchors aweigh, my boys," and we ...*

TAKE THE NEXT STEP

What things do you feel you "gotta" have in place in your life before you can seriously write? Do you realize it's possible for you to seriously write without any of these, other than a pen and paper?

FRESHMAN-ITIS

You're a high school freshman. Write from this low-man-on-the-totem-pole perspective. Be a teenager!

Use these initials to create a name: M.P.K. ______

A NICKNAME: ______ EYE COLOR: ______

HAIR COLOR: ______ NICKNAMES OF BEST FRIENDS: ______

HOW YOUR BEST FRIENDS TREAT YOU: ______

HOW YOU TREAT YOUR BEST FRIENDS: ______

FAVORITE FOOD: ______ THOUGHTS ON SPORTS: ______

SOMETHING ABOUT YOUR LOCKER: ______

Start with: *It hasn't been the best day, but it certainly hasn't been the worst …*

TAKE THE NEXT STEP

Not every day can be the "best" day. Write one affirmative thing about your creative self from the last twenty-four hours.

If you like this exercise, get a notebook (or open a new file) and keep an affirmation journal where you can record something positive about yourself for the day—every day.

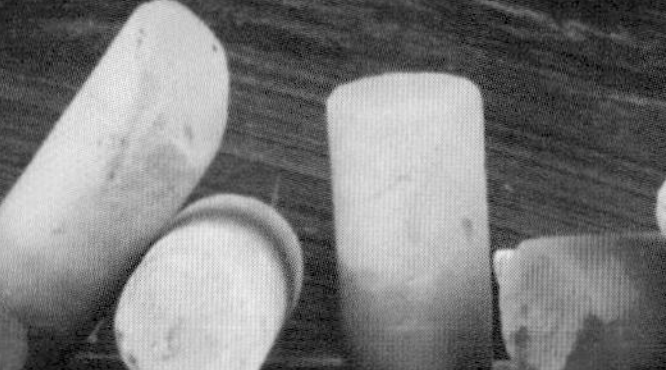

PEEPHOLE 3

You look through the peephole of your front door and see Santa Claus. Write the story. Start with: *It's not that I don't believe ...*

TAKE THE NEXT STEP

How does sticking to the exercises in this book fit into the "big picture" of your life?

THOSE WERE THE DAYS

Finish the story. Start with: *Back in 1938, before ...*

TAKE THE NEXT STEP

If there are 1,938 reasons *not* to write, name one reason *to* write that outweighs them all.

So what are you waiting for? See how much you can write before the year 2038!

WEIRD WORDS

Use the words *atmu* and *bukra* in your story—even though you probably don't know what they mean. Set your story in Alaska in December. Start with: *Lapis sky, green palms, sand the color of pale gold ...*

TAKE THE NEXT STEP

If you think Alaska in December is cold, imagine how you're treating yourself when you belittle what you've written. Read aloud (in a nice, warm, gentle tone) what you just wrote. Tell yourself (aloud) all the things you like about it: striking imagery, good word choice, nice handwriting, clever ending, etc. Do this with everything you write!

(*Atmu* is Egyptian for "twilight," and *bukra* is Egyptian for "tomorrow.")

Gifted

Finish the story. Start with: *Here's a photo from my second birthday, where I preferred the wrapping paper over the ...*

TAKE THE NEXT STEP

Think out of the box and compare what you just wrote ...

... to a gift.

... to being sixteen.

... to a kumquat.

TIME WARP

Think of an era you would like to be from (past or future). Give yourself a new name from this time, using your current initials. If you think you also should be of the opposite sex, make that change, too.

New Name: ______________________ Current age: ______

What do you spend your days doing? ______________________

Who is the closest person to you? ______________________

What is your favorite possession? ______________________

You are now this character. Write from his or her perspective. Start with: *It was so close I could taste it ...*

TAKE THE NEXT STEP

If you could travel back in time, what one writing moment would you relive? Why? You just did. Hope you enjoyed it!

WORD WOK

List five foreign words here (make sure you know the meaning of the words):

1. __________
2. __________
3. __________
4. __________
5. __________

Use all five words in a story that takes place on a new planet. Begin with the phrase: *It was a crescent-shaped moon ...*

TAKE THE NEXT STEP

Think of four words or expressions that are used by your family or the people where you grew up (example: "Outten the lights") and write them here:

1. __________
2. __________
3. __________
4. __________

This is a great way to add local color to your writing. Use all four in a mini-autobiography.

TEN PENS

Each of the ten pens in the alley on this page has a word on it. When you read them, they form a sentence. Start with the given phrase at the top of the alley and cover the entire alley with your writing, incorporating the words or word sets as you get to them. Try to make each word set fall naturally into a story that is not about bowling or shoes.

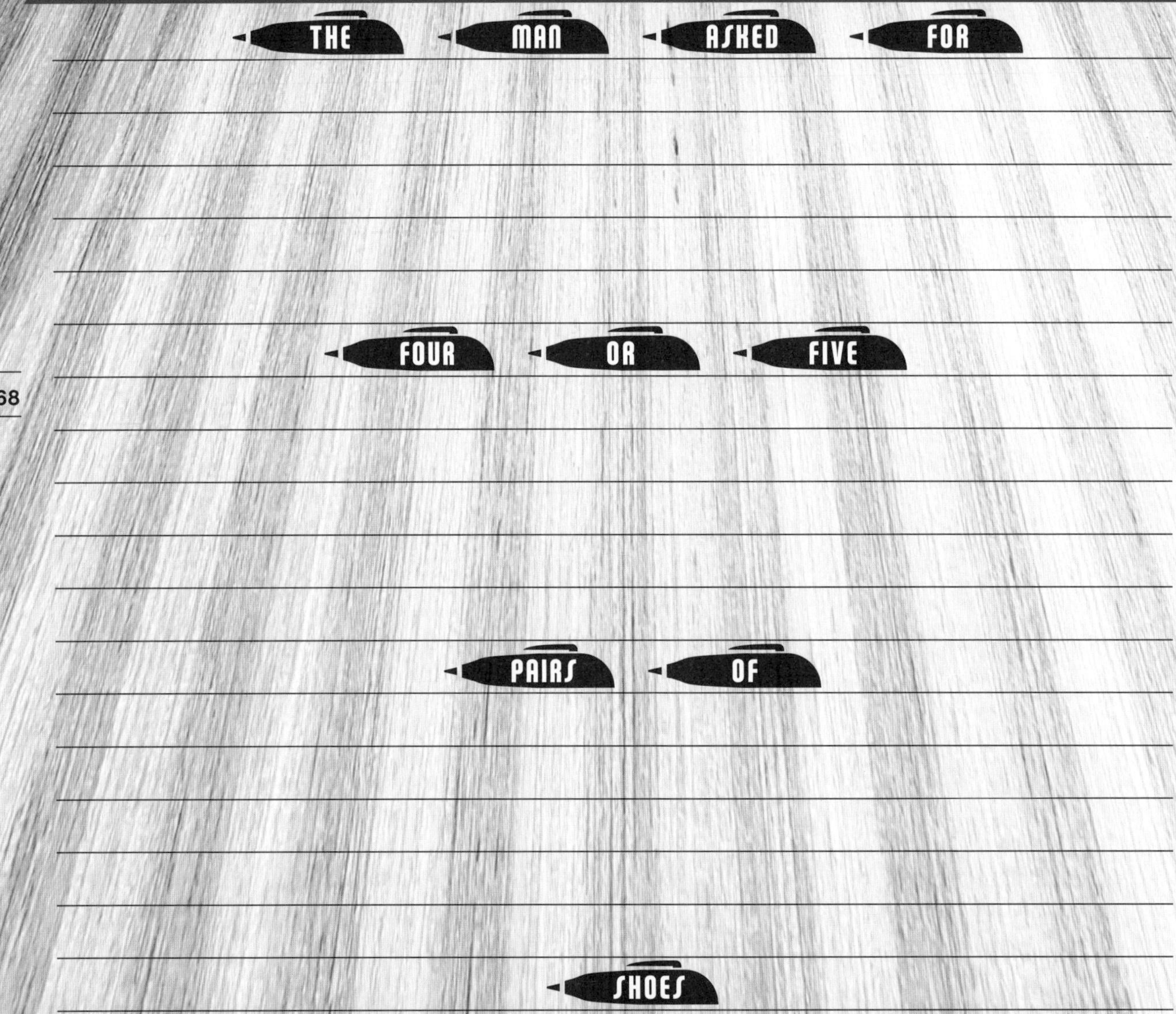

TAKE THE NEXT STEP

Don't you just love the bumpers that keep bowling balls out of the gutter, guaranteeing kids will knock down at least a few pins? Writing exercises are a lot like those bumpers. They make writing fun while also providing a safe space to explore the craft. Unlike bumpers, you don't need to worry about outgrowing writing exercises. Writers of all levels use them for getting unblocked, warming up, fleshing out characters or scenes, and generating new ideas for projects. And you don't even need ten pens—just one pen and ten minutes. Make sure you schedule time into your day for writing exercises.

Triple Play

For this exercise set a timer for ten minutes. You will spend three minutes each on three short pieces. For each one, choose one of the three starters provided. The speed at which you write will not give you any time to think, so your inner critic won't have a chance to rear its head. After nine minutes of writing, take the last minute to read all three pieces aloud, underlining a total of three words, phrases, or other structural items that please your ear. In future writings, try to use similar words, techniques, and structures.

1 At the playground ... Brick by brick ... In the end ...

2 Men in uniform ... The teakettle whistled ... When a seagull ...

3 Through the haze ... The piggy bank ... The onion rings ...

TAKE THE NEXT STEP

The top three criteria for setting achievable goals: (1) Make them measurable so you know when you actually have accomplished them, (2) make them realistic so they are a stretch but within reach, and (3) share them with others so you stay accountable. Write your top three writing goals here. Look at them every day to keep them in the forefront of your consciousness—it will help make them happen.

1. ____________________
2. ____________________
3. ____________________

GENDER BENDER

If you are female, write as if you are a retired male New York police officer who lives with ten cats. If you are male, write as if you are a retired female receptionist from New York who lives with twenty cats.

Start with: *I remember that day in July when it hailed ...*

TAKE THE NEXT STEP

Do you have preconceived judgments about yourself that get in the way of writing? Tomorrow when you write, choose to be a nonjudgmental blank slate. See what comes.

Finish the story.

It was a sunny May morning when I awoke with a special spring in my step. Somehow, overnight, I had merged with a coil and was able to do all sorts of things other humans could not. For instance, when I ...

TAKE THE NEXT STEP

For writers, spring is the perfect time to write Christmas, Hanukkah, and New Year's articles for print magazines, since many publications acquire these pieces four to six months in advance. Jot down some article ideas for publication two seasons from now. Now write one! Thank goodness for the shorter deadlines of online publications—it's not easy to hum Christmas carols while sweltering through the dog days of summer.

CLOSED ENCOUNTERS

You are now going to write with your eyes closed. You may find it helpful to use your nonwriting hand to support or guide your movement down the page.

Start with: *I don't see why ...*

TAKE THE NEXT STEP

Name one facet of your writing for which you'd like to seek support. What is keeping you from asking for help? Debunk the reasoning behind not asking. Now reach out for that help or support.

FIVE-AND-TEN

Pick the number of today's date, and locate it below. This is a five-word starter for your writing. If you like, use it to flesh out characters from your "regular" writing.

1 In a big yellow plastic	2 At the center of town	3 Bright flashes of neon light	4 Hired as a security guard	5 He broke into a trot	6 He always had chapped lips	7 She quickly let go of
8 The old brass key was	9 At Tooth Fairy training school	10 Also known as Cheerful Charlie	11 He left without saying goodbye	12 Yelling into the bullhorn she	13 Holding on for dear life	14 In the window seat was
15 With an air of mystery	16 I have a weakness for	17 The smell of summer rain	18 Always stuck in the outfield	19 I was having trouble seeing	20 It happened so fast that	21 We sat on the stoop
22 Life on a windmill farm	23 Measure twice and cut once	24 Missing his two front teeth	25 Not exactly a con artist	26 Saturday mornings in the barbershop	27 The most precious of the	28 In my great grandmother's kitchen
29 Her first experience changing a	30 Donning a black cape, she	31 She clicked her chewing gum				

TAKE THE NEXT STEP

When I was a kid, the place to buy inexpensive toys was the five-and-ten; now it's the dollar store. A stroll through one will net you some interesting writing ideas. Here are a few for you, all of which came to me on my last trip to the dollar store:

1. A nun buying twelve cans of Goofy String Spray, thirty plastic ice cream cone holders, and a pair of earbuds.
2. A little boy crying at the top of his lungs because his mother won't buy him a plastic fireman's hat.
3. An elderly woman yelling across the frozen food aisle to her husband, "George, you gotta start eatin' better like Doc said. You wanna get some of these fish sticks?"

Listing

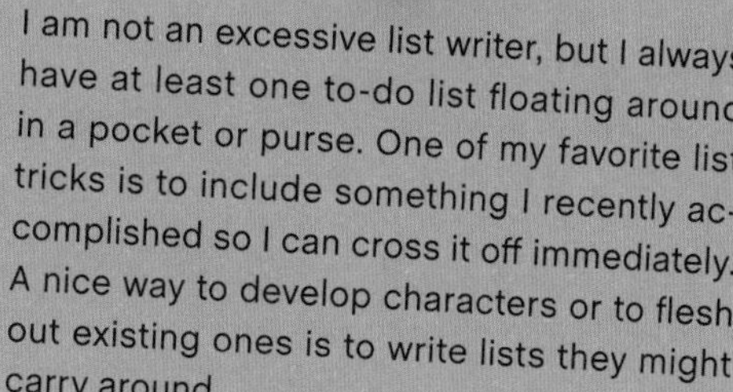

I am not an excessive list writer, but I always have at least one to-do list floating around in a pocket or purse. One of my favorite list tricks is to include something I recently accomplished so I can cross it off immediately. A nice way to develop characters or to flesh out existing ones is to write lists they might carry around.

Choose a character:

1. A retired high school French teacher
2. A crossword puzzle constructor
3. A single mother of three
4. A recently divorced fifty-year-old man
5. A waitress

What entries would his or her lists contain? Here are some ideas to get you started:

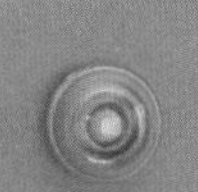

List this character's top two New Year's resolutions.

List this character's current shopping list.

List this character's five things that are always put off.

List this character's most pressing calls, e-mails, or texts that have to be returned.

List this character's top two places to visit.

List this character's top three chores/errands for this weekend.

After completing the lists, if you'd like to breathe even more life into this character, write from his or her point of view and start with the phrase, *The boat was listing starboard ....*

TAKE THE NEXT STEP

One way to identify who you are as a writer is to list all of your writing dreams on a piece of paper. Create your own wishing well to hold your dreams by taking a container that pleases you and placing the list in it. As new writing dreams come to you, place them in the container. It will hold on to them while you work towards them, one at a time.

the WHO

First, pick the narrator of this story:

A young child

A sickly person

A blind person

A deaf person

A mute person

A ninety-nine-year-old person

A teenager

A once wealthy, now poor, person

A nouveau riche person

A street person

Now write a story, as told by your narrator, that includes the following three things:

1. Chocolate
2. A kiss
3. A song that is important to you

Start with: *This is a story about ...*

TAKE THE NEXT STEP

Determining when to use *who*, the subject of a verb, and *whom*, the object form of a pronoun (as in *Who/whom should I ask about the sale?*) is easy if you follow a simple trick: Answer the question or restate the sentence using *he* or *him*. If the answer or restate uses *he*, then the correct word is *who*. If the answer or restate uses *him*, then the correct word is *whom*. Who/whom should I ask about the sale? You should ask *him*. Because the answer included the word *him*, the correct word to use is *whom*.

STREAMING IMAGES

Using an image as your starting point, you will write a stream-of-consciousness list of everything you think of, letting one word or phrase lead to the next as your mind wanders and makes associations. Don't filter anything. Write the first thing that comes to mind. Write until something jumps out at you as a good topic for a timed writing. Then run with it.

Here's an example:

camp counselor, camp photo, skinned knee, sunburn, Virginia Beach, family vacation, Williamsburg, getting my sisters lost.

I would stop writing here so I could write the story about getting my sisters lost in Williamsburg, Virginia.

Pick an image from which you will begin a stream-of-consciousness list. Then grab a separate sheet of paper and run with it.

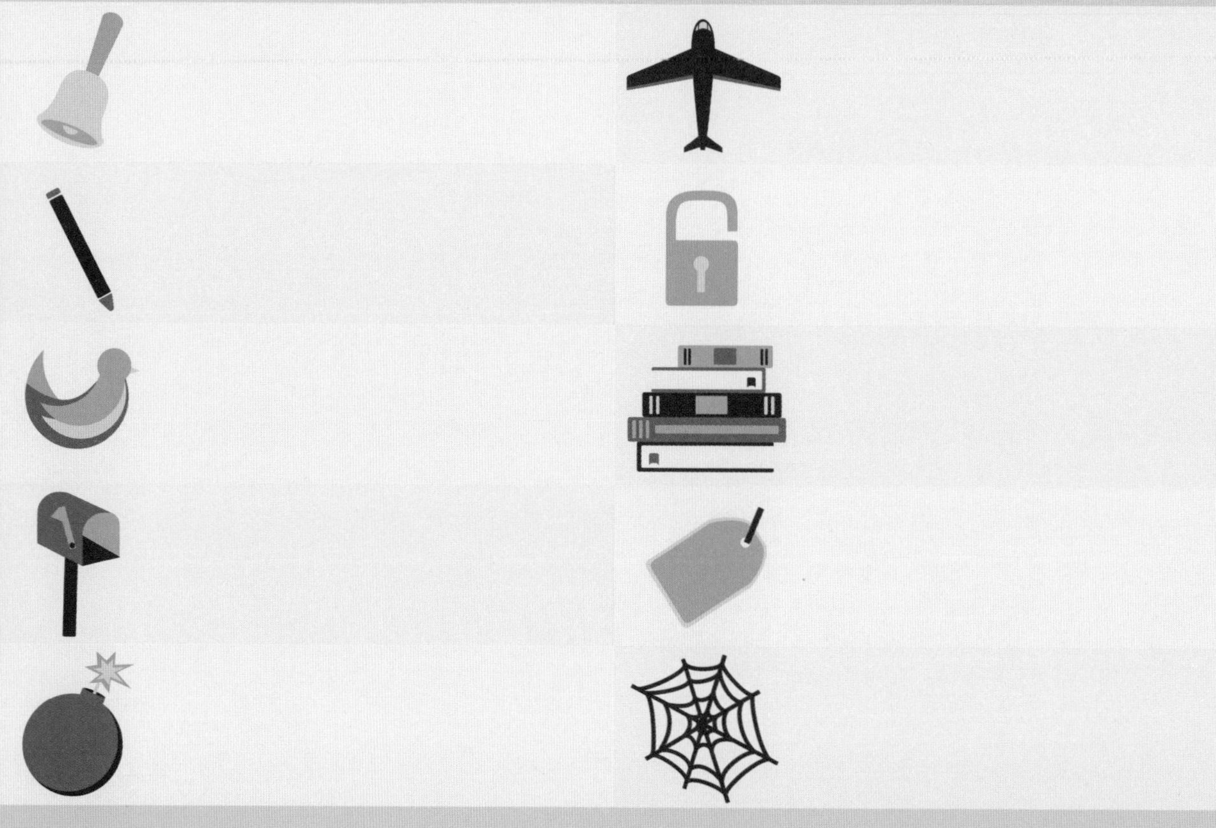

TAKE THE NEXT STEP

To create this exercise, I skimmed through many clip-art images. One that didn't translate well when I shrunk it down was a seven-day compartmentalized pill holder. If you have one, dig it out. Write a different writing goal or task on seven slips of paper, and put one in each compartment. Leave the holder in the bathroom, and open it every morning when you brush your teeth. Carry the goal with you all day until you reach it. As soon as it's done, write a new goal on a new slip of paper and place it into the same compartment for the following week.

GENDER BENDER

2

If you are male, write as if you are a female hairdresser who works from the basement of her home in New Jersey. If you are female, write as if you are a retired male ranch hand who lives above a drugstore in Montana.

Start with: *The emergency room ...*

TAKE THE NEXT STEP

The emergence of a new idea is a wonderful feeling. Describe how it feels to you.

Equate this with something concrete (like a perfect pirouette or riding the world's tallest roller coaster). Get a picture of this, and keep it in your wallet to remind you of your creativity.

ANIMAL TENDENCIES

Think of an animal you relate to. Use mental images of this animal as you work through this exercise. Fill in the blanks to create a piece of poetic prose.

The animal inside me wears ... ______________________

He or she is afraid of ... ______________________

And eats only ... ______________________

____

The animal inside me despises ... ______________________

He or she lives in ... ______________________

And plays with ... ______________________

____

The animal inside me sings ... ______________________

He or she has a collection of ... ______________________

And revels in ... ______________________

____

The animal inside me loves ... ______________________

He or she is waiting for ... ______________________

And wishes that ... ______________________

____

And sometimes, when no one is looking, the animal inside me ... ______________________

____

____

TAKE THE NEXT STEP

When you are in the flow of writing, to which animal are you most similar? What are its traits? Keep a picture of this animal handy. Looking at it before and while you write will help you get into deeper writing faster.

ELEMENTS, DEAR WATSON

Write four shorts about the elements. Be as metaphorical as you like. Use the starters provided.

The earth sounds ...

The wind looks ...

The rain tastes ...

The fire smells ...

TAKE THE NEXT STEP

One more. *The act of writing feels ...* ______

SCRIBBLE • ONE

This exercise uses letter tiles like those found in a familiar word-based board game. When you get to a letter and use it as the *first letter* of a word, you get two points. Try for fifty points!

His eyes ...

D

O

Q

A I

A

R

R

R

I H

G

V

M Z

M

N

E E

Y O

E

R

T U

TAKE THE NEXT STEP

A good way to flex your writing muscles is to play word games or work on puzzles. Decode this cryptogram (a quote that has been encrypted by a single letter substitution) from author and professor Mary Gordon:

K ITYXBT AWBW K CZATJKV XZ XTL ZAX XUB JBI WXBS YJ HTZJX ZH XUB FYTTZT.

(Answer: A writer uses a journal to try out the new step in front of the mirror.)

Free to Bee

Start with the word *bee* and free-associate. Write down whatever comes to mind.

Bee

Circle a few interesting words. Use them in a story about a recently freed prisoner. Start with: *I have been ...*

TAKE THE NEXT STEP

Write a story idea here:

Free-associate ideas from it on a separate sheet of paper. Did you find a topic you like better?

Moral • Two

Use the moral at the bottom of the page to conclude the story you are about to write.

Start with: *The turtle-slow truck ...*

And the moral is: *One man's ceiling is another man's floor.*

TAKE THE NEXT STEP

Imagine the "writer" part of your personality floating up to the ceiling and looking down at the rest of you. What would he or she tell you to help you be a better writer?

Belly Dancer Beliefs

You are a belly dancer. Complete each of these four shorts in her voice.

Guns are ...

The right to ...

Stephen King is ...

Republicans are ...

TAKE THE NEXT STEP

Where do your characters come from? Combine two people you know—one relative and one friend—to come up with a new character. The next time you write, use this character's point of view.

Revenge of the Journal

You are the journal or diary of an eighteen-year-old girl. She's been writing in you daily about dieting, school, her ex–best friend, an upcoming dance, and one particular boy. You're tired of her complaints and her whining. So while she is asleep one night, you write back.

Dear ____________________,

It has been ... ____________________

TAKE THE NEXT STEP

Write a one-sentence journal entry in observation of your writing process.

If you like this exercise, keep a separate process journal in which you record daily thoughts about your writing process. (Thanks to Rachel Simon, author of *Riding the Bus with My Sister* and *The Story of Beautiful Girl*, for this helpful idea.)

Finish the story. Start with: *At an early age, the little boy discovered ...*

TAKE THE NEXT STEP

Do you think you might possess some creative talents you have yet to discover? List some possibilities. Commit to exploring one of these in the next three months. What first step will you take towards this commitment?

REBUS TERMINAL

Instead of words, this exercise involves symbols. Use them as you come to them. Start with: *The bus pulled into the terminal in ...*

TAKE THE NEXT STEP

Imagine taking the bus tour of your writing dreams. List the top three writing accomplishments you'd like to visit within the next year.

If you're gonna hop on the bus, Gus, it behooves you to write every day!

Keyed UP

Use all these words.

messed blessed caressed pressed recessed stressed

Start with: *I was all keyed up ...*

TAKE THE NEXT STEP

Describe a person you know who does everything slowly and methodically. Write at their slow speed. If this describes you, write about yourself, but write really fast.

Try a new pace the next time you write.

SNAPSHOTS ONE

Photos are a great way to capture memories, but we're writers, so we can do the same thing just by using words. Write quick "word snapshots" as photo substitutes for the topics on this page. Try to capture colors, textures, and expressions. Use your own life story … or make them up!

A childhood birthday party:

TAKE THE NEXT STEP

If someone took a snapshot of you while you were writing today, what would the caption read? Now write a caption for a snapshot taken while you are deeply entrenched in the flow of writing. Make this caption a reality when you write tomorrow.

Winning something:

A wedding:

A garden:

FRANCE WITH NO PANTS

You have just won a free two-day trip to France, but there's a catch: You must leave immediately. There's no time to go home and pack. All you can bring is what you are wearing and carrying with you today. Plus, you are given fif-teen minutes and $55 to spend at an airport store. What do you buy, if anything?

Tell the story of your adventure to the person sitting next to you on the return flight home. Start with: *What a whirlwind ...*

TAKE THE NEXT STEP

Many writers are adrenaline junkies, only able to create when pressure is on or the muse is screaming in their ear. Where do you get your energy and motivation to write? Is there something different you'd like to try? Like what?

Write the names of six flowers, and then use all six in your writing. Think creatively: *Daisy* could be a woman's name, and *rose* could be a color.

Start with: *Never one to remember things like ...*

TAKE THE NEXT STEP

The more specific you are in your writing, the more your reader will get a vivid picture in her imagination. Try your hand at this one: Describe a rose as if it was an oil painting done with words.

DRIBBLING BANANAS

List eight action verbs from sports, all ending in *-ing*:

1.
2.
3.
4.
5.
6.
7.
8.

List eight everyday plural nouns:

1.
2.
3.
4.
5.
6.
7.
8.

Now draw arrows connecting these verbs and nouns in unusual combinations. You'll end up with things like *dribbling bananas*, *squatting shoes*, *shooting lima beans*, etc. Pick one (or more) of these combinations, and use the images in a story that begins: *The alarm went off ...*

TAKE THE NEXT STEP

Have you written "morning pages" as per Julia Cameron's book *The Artist's Way*? It's a great way to clear your mind so nothing stands between you and your creativity for the rest of the day. Put a pen and three sheets of paper by the alarm clock. As soon as the alarm goes off, write until all three pages are filled. Observe the differences you feel during the rest of the day.

CLOSED ENCOUNTERS

THE SEQUEL

Earlier in this book you had the chance to write with your eyes closed. Now that you have mastered this, you are going to write with your eyes closed again, but this time you will use your nondominant hand. You may find it helpful once again to use your dominant hand to guide your movement down the page. Start with: *Every time I see ...*

TAKE THE NEXT STEP

Sometimes when we're in the thick of writing a long work, the middle gets muddy and we can't see our way out. The middle can have just as much energy as the beginning or end. Case in point: Oreo cookies or a peanut butter and jelly sandwich. Think of other things that have wonderful middles, and compare them to your writing process.

LOVE LETTER STORY

Make up a sentence, or the beginning of a sentence, containing words beginning with the following letters: T, S, L, M, A, B. Examples: *Tracy Stone loved marbles and baubles ...* . Or *The sprite leprechaun missed a beat ...* . Use this sentence or phrase as a beginning for a story.

T ____________ S ____________ L ____________ M ____________

A ____________ B ____________

(*Love Story* by Erich Segal begins with words with these six letters: "That she loved Mozart and Bach ...")

TAKE THE NEXT STEP

What do you love about reading? Everything you read was created by a writer. You, too, have the talent and commitment to bring this joy to others. Keep writing and you will give more folks more reasons to love reading.

POST CARDS

WITHOUT PICTURES

You are at the described location, sending a postcard to the specified person. Write a message using each of these prompts.

TAKE THE NEXT STEP

What one thing about your writing practice currently makes you proud?

Write this on a postcard, address it to yourself, and mail it. When it arrives, hang it on the refrigerator like you would a picture postcard sent to you from a dear friend.

QUOTA OF QUOTES

Use as many of the following Ben Franklin quotes in your story as you can:

★ A penny saved is a penny earned. ★ A stitch in time saves nine. ★ Eat to live, and not live to eat. ★
★ Some are weatherwise, some are otherwise. ★ An empty bag cannot stand upright. ★
★ The used key is always bright. ★ Lost time is never found again. ★ The cat in gloves catches no mice. ★

☞ Start with: *Not to sound like my …*

☞ TAKE THE NEXT STEP

When I don't get my quota of creative time, I feel a bit ornery and out of sorts. How do you feel when you're not following your passion? Why perpetuate this neglect? Choose one thing you can change right away.

CAPTAIN of CAPTIVATING CAPTIONS

When traveling through very small towns, I love to buy local newspapers. My favorite stories are about local residents who have done something extraordinary or, perhaps a better way of putting it, out of the ordinary. Usually a photograph of this person in all his glory (or shame) appears with it. You are now a writer for such a paper. There's a catch—you didn't attend the event. Rather, you are handed a photograph. From it, you must write a caption, the article about what happened that made it newsworthy, and a headline.

Pick a description of the photograph you were given.

1. A person whose face is covered in something, perhaps some sort of food
2. An enormous pig
3. A kid with no front teeth
4. A person who might be nude standing partially behind a huge boulder
5. A person with a tomato in hand

TAKE THE NEXT STEP

When writing captions, assume the reader will look at the picture and its caption without ever reading the full story. A good caption is brief, yet manages to cover as much of the "who, what, when, where, why, and how" as possible. Use a writing style that reflects the picture and the venue in which it appears, and always check your facts—twice!

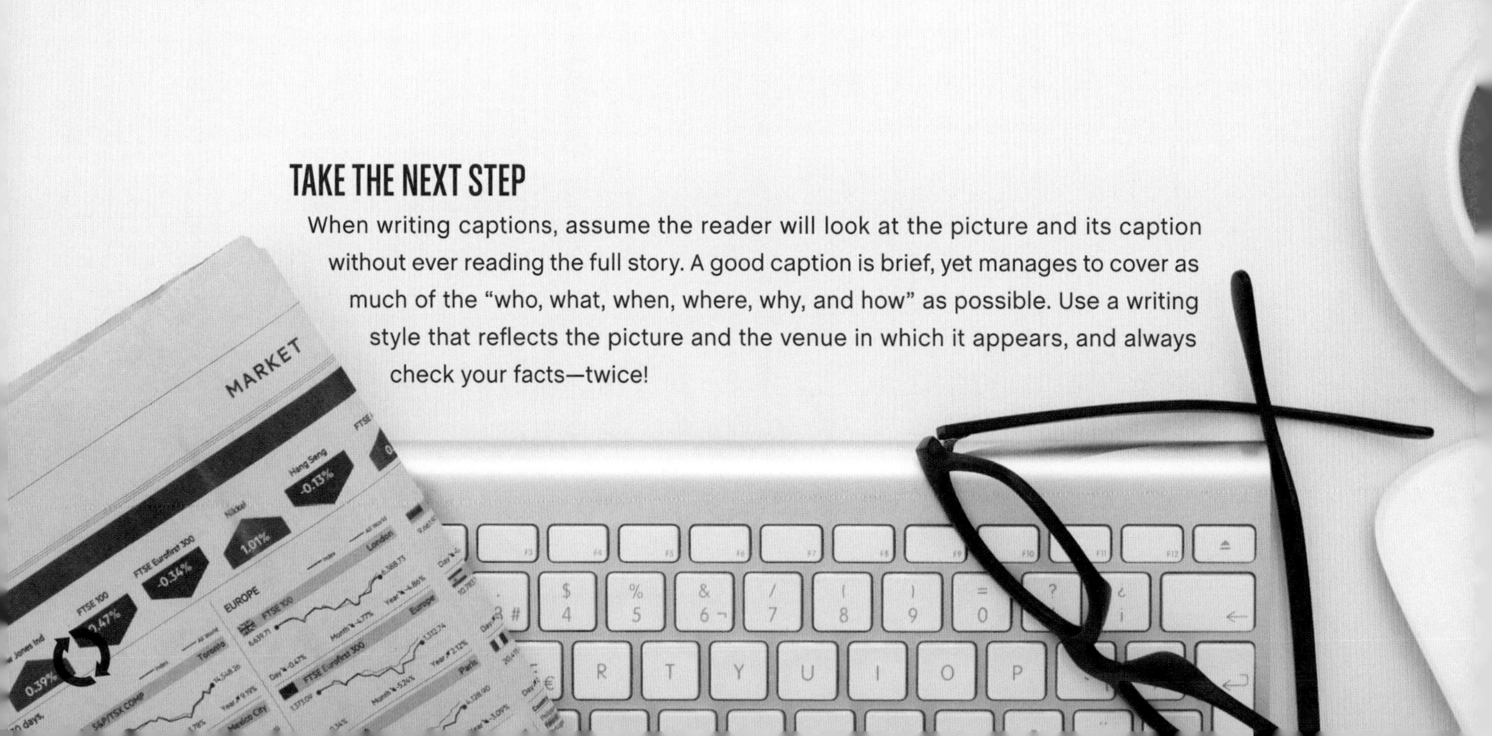

Hear, Hear 1

Finish the story. Start with: *The first time I heard about him, I had a feeling ...*

TAKE THE NEXT STEP

The next time you sit down to write and you hear silence instead of your muse, immediately write, starting with the phrase, "I don't hear ..." Try it now.

Hear, Hear 2

Finish the story. Start with: *From the second I heard about her I knew ...*

TAKE THE NEXT STEP

Write about the moment you realized that writing was work but you loved it anyway. If this never happened to you, make it up.

Finish the story.

For the fourth hour in a row she stared at the blank ...

TAKE THE NEXT STEP

If a tree is recognized by its fruit, what is it about your writing style that makes it easily recognizable and unique to readers?

Fictionary•One

Write a dictionary-style definition for *cinchonism*, pronounced "SING-ke-NIZ-um."

Use *cinchonism* with your fictitious definition in a story. Start with: *The stars were …*

The real definition of *cinchonism*: a pathological condition resulting from an overdose of cinchona bark, a tree/shrub native to the Andes whose bark yields quinine. How close was your definition?

TAKE THE NEXT STEP

Writing is not just output; it's also input. Have you ever gone skydiving, or spoken in front of a thousand people? List some things you'd like to experience.

Schedule one of these things now for the sake of your craft.

Verrrrrrrrry Sleeeeeeepy

Write, and whenever you get to a word, use it!

Start with: *The hypnotist promised he could help ...*

circles

stairs

huge

tiny

sparkle

ice

fire

alarm

spiral

TAKE THE NEXT STEP

You've been hypnotized to drop whatever you are doing every morning at exactly seven o'clock and write for seven minutes. Try it out.

Metamorphosis

Finish the story. Start with: *Like a butterfly, she magically …*

TAKE THE NEXT STEP

If you treated all your creative desires and demands as if you were a butterfly, what would you do differently?

The next time you write, spread your wings and see how your writing changes.

DEFECTIVE DETECTIVE

What is the oddest thing someone would find in one of the drawers in your home or office? What's the item? Which drawer? You are a detective investigating a case, and you come across this item. Of course, it belongs to someone you've never met and is in a place you've never been before. What would you conclude about this unknown person and his or her life? Start with: *Hidden under ...*

TAKE THE NEXT STEP

Everyone's an expert at something, whether it's being a detective or picking the ripest cantaloupe. List some of your more unusual areas of expertise. Can you turn one or more into a writing project?

Autograph

Write about getting an autograph from a famous person whom you've idolized for a long time. Use these five words or phrases in your story: *fly swatter, scale, rye bread, law, ebony*. Start with: *I always carry a pen with me, except for the time ...*

TAKE THE NEXT STEP

TV shows have spin-offs; movies have sequels. What are some current or complete projects you can turn into sidebars or articles? How can you spin off one of the exercises in this book and turn it into an article or an op-ed?

HOT AND BOTHERED

1

Write eight action words (verbs) that end in *-ing* down the left column. Write eight colors in the right column.

1	1
2	2
3	3
4	4
5	5
6	6
7	7
8	8

2

Now make up two new expressions:

1. One that starts with one of the verbs and ends with one of the colors (like "running orange"):

2. One that starts with one of the colors and ends with one of the verbs (like "green stretching"):

3

Use both expressions in a story. Start with: *It was sweltering yellow hot ...*

TAKE THE NEXT STEP

On snow days, we take the day off work and devote time instead to eating, playing, and accomplishing very little. Why don't we do the same when it's unbearably hot? Today, no matter what the weather, take a heat day. Get a cool drink, sit back, and fan yourself. If, while relaxing, you come up with writing ideas, jot them down.

PreQuills are actions or questions to contemplate before you write. They help keep your goals at the front of your mind, bring you into the present, and make sure you get good value for your writing time. For this exercise, you may choose to write down the answers or merely think them; both approaches work. Choose from one of these PreQuills.

1. Slowly breathe in and out through your nose ten times while keeping count so your mind has something to focus on. Then answer this question: *For whom am I writing today?*
2. Answer this: *What is my writing goal today?* With the answer in mind, write until you accomplish it. Then write one more sentence so you can exceed your goal.
3. Think about a time when you felt great joy from writing. Relive the entire episode. With this great feeling present in your heart and mind once again, pick up your pen to write.
4. Jump up and down and clap your hands above your head ten times. With energy flowing into your hands, answer this: *What about writing energizes me?*
5. Think about someone who is a fan of yours. Answer this: *What words does she use to describe my writing?* Let the words soak in. Do not negate them. They are true.
6. Think of a place where you love to write. What does it smell like? What are its sounds? What have you eaten there? What tactile things come to mind? Write from this place.

Now that you have done your PreQuill, your mind is in the present and your pen is primed. Use this as an opportunity to write! Start with: *I guarded ...*

TAKE THE NEXT STEP

A PostScript is the opposite of a PreQuill. After you've completed your writing session, jot down a positive comment about the day's writing. Keep these comments in a notebook or little box. Before you write again, take a look at some of your PostScripts to quickly get back in the zone. If you do, you'll have an ever-growing batch of PreQuills to add to your repertoire.

Corner Pocket

Finish this story. Start with: *At the bottom of our street is Town Pool, known for ...*

TAKE THE NEXT STEP

Wander around in search of an action worth recording (done by another person, an animal, Mother Nature, etc.). Describe it in detail. If you like, keep a mini-notebook in your pocket and record one observed action daily until you fill the book.

CUBISM

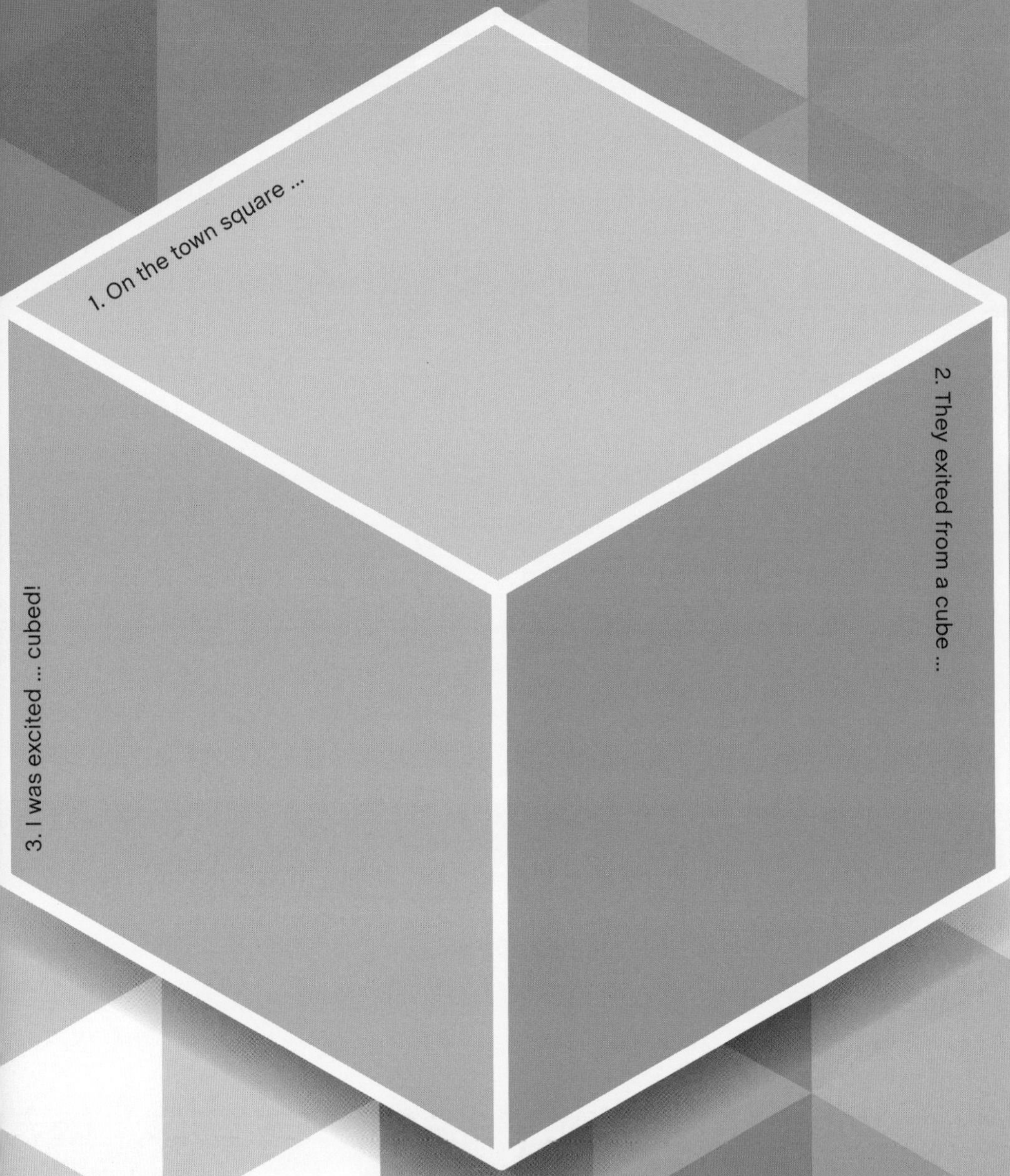

□ □ □ □ □ □ □

Using the starter on section 1, write until you fill the parallelogram. Rotate the page and continue the story with the starter in section 2. When you fill that parallelogram, turn the paper one last time until section 3 is on top. Use its starter to complete the story as you fill in the box shape.

□ □ □ □ □ □ □

TAKE THE NEXT STEP

Have you ever played "The Cube" imagination game from the book by Annie Gottlieb and Slobodan D. Pešić? Here's a small sample for you to try: You are walking alone in a desert, and you come upon a cube. Answer these questions: *How big is the cube? What color is the cube? How does the color make you feel? How far is the cube from you? Can you see inside the cube? How big is the cube compared to the desert?* The cube represents you and how you see yourself in the world. The filled-in cube on this page represents your commitment to being a writer. How does it feel when you call yourself a writer? Exciting^3?

□ □ □ □ □ □ □

Finish the story. Start with: *He was a little bit rock and roll and a little bit ...*

TAKE THE NEXT STEP

Even when you're stuck in traffic, there are creative writing exercises you can do! Think of the first line of a song you really like. Come up with new lyrics for second and third lines.

Squeaky Wheel

Write down six sounds or noises that kids' toys make:

1. ____________________
2. ____________________
3. ____________________
4. ____________________
5. ____________________
6. ____________________

Use as many of these sounds as you can in a story starting with: *The laser beam penetrated ...*

TAKE THE NEXT STEP

Write a quick note from your fifteen-years-from-now self to your present self. Assure yourself that something that seems like a big squeaky creative problem now will turn out to be a minor laser blip on the screen of your writing life.

The Great Inquisition

Fill in the blanks with the first word that comes to mind:

A landmark: ____________________

An article of clothing: ____________

A cooking verb: _________________

A beverage: ____________________

A planet: ______________________

A word about glass: _____________

TAKE THE NEXT STEP

If you met up with your playful five-year-old self, what one question would you like to ask him or her about creativity? How do you think he or she would answer?

Use these six words in your story. Start with: *I remember asking ...*

NUMB NUMBERS

Wherever you come to a number on the page, use it in your story. Start with, *While under anesthesia, I ...*

4

222

3,142

16

0

771

TAKE THE NEXT STEP

On a 1 to 100 percent scale of currently available time that you could use to write, what percent of this time do you actually spend writing? What nonwriting activity could you do less to bring this writing percent up a couple percentage points? Try it, and see what happens.

WINTER OF MY DISC & TENT

Finish the story ...

After I finished recording my album, I hit the road to sell it. With barely enough money to make ends meet, I decided to camp in my old scouting tent. My first stop, on February 1, was Des Moines, Iowa, where I met a girl who ...

TAKE THE NEXT STEP ▶▶

Brainstorm some names as if you were starting a writing business or a business that incorporates your writing talents. Make sure it describes who you are and what you do.

Flavor of the Month

Write down twelve flavors:

Use all twelve flavors in this piece. Start with: *The sparkling water was ...*

TAKE THE NEXT STEP

Sending marshmallow-fudge-swirl-double-cone prose to an editor whose preference is a small dish of lime sorbet poetry usually results in a rejection. List publications and publishers with whom your writing flavors and portions are compatible. Send your writing to one of them.

Different Directions

Use the words as you get to them. Start with: *The first time I sat on the ...*

north

northeast

southeast

south

west

southwest

northwest

east

TAKE THE NEXT STEP

Like life, sometimes our writing takes a very different turn from what we had intended or expected. Write positively about the direction your writing is now headed.

REMINISCING·TWO

Imagine talking to a friend from your childhood. Retell and reminisce about favorite times. Use the starting phrases provided.

Do you remember the time we tried ...

Do you remember the time we wrote ...

Do you remember the time we were asked ...

Do you remember the time we quit ...

TAKE THE NEXT STEP

If you don't bring your ideas to life by writing them, they will become well-kept secrets. When you're writing, imagine you are sharing with a childhood friend. Let your pen breathe life into the first sentence of an idea now.

TWO LIFE SENTENCES

Use these two sentences about life in your story:

1. Life is like drawing without an eraser. —Anonymous
2. Life shrinks or expands in proportion to one's courage. —Anaïs Nin

Start with: *The bloody ...* ______

TAKE THE NEXT STEP

When it comes to life, are you a mental pre-planner? A spontaneous jump-right-in-er? A plodder? A the-present-is-a-gift-er? A procrastinator? A lamenter of missed chances?

How is this reflected in your writing practice?

Snooping

Think back to a time when you peeped in someplace that you shouldn't have. One example might be looking in the drawer of the nightstand of the people you were babysitting for. Write about this episode, embellishing to your heart's content if you like, and tell what you found! Start with: *When I opened ...*

Opening lines must grab the reader on many levels. Go back through this book, and choose an opening line you wrote. Rewrite it, and then polish it until it shines.

Moral Three

Use the moral at the bottom of the page to conclude the story you are about to write. Start with: *She watched the sky ...*

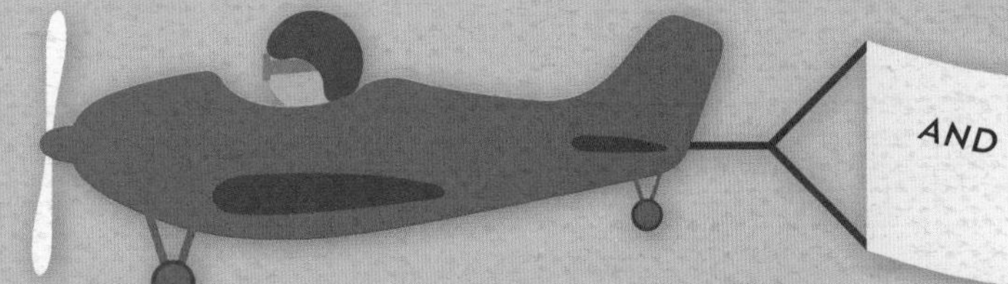

AND THE MORAL OF THE STORY: THE BIGGER THEY COME, THE HARDER THEY FALL.

TAKE THE NEXT STEP

Could you pick your inner critic out of a lineup? What would you convict him or her of? What sentence (allow the pun to influence your answer) does he or she deserve? Is it true that "the bigger they come, the harder they fall"?

LOOK MA ... TWO HANDS!

Quick! Go get a second writing implement. For this exercise, you are going to write with both hands at the same time. To make it a little easier on you and your brain, you'll be using the same starting phrase and writing the same words (while you use both hands at the same time!).

On this side of the page, write with your *left* hand:
When the hot air balloon ...

On this side, use your *right* hand:
When the hot air balloon ...

TAKE THE NEXT STEP

Imagine shaking hands with a writer you adore. What does he or she see in your eyes?

AMBIGUOUS

Use this ambiguous sentence in a story: *Mary was cooking in the pot.*
Start with: *I could have used a kick in the seat of the pants the day that ...*

TAKE THE NEXT STEP

Make believe your writing is something you cooked. Write a rave review for it like a food or restaurant critic would. Use this as a motivational kick in the pants the next time your writing practice wanes.

HANG-UPS

You are a fifty-eight-year-old nurse who is a hypochondriac and works in a doctor's office. Write from this perspective.

Start with: *I hung up on him twice ...*

TAKE THE NEXT STEP

We all have hang-ups about some facets of grammar. List two of yours:

1. __________
2. __________

Now find a book or information on the Internet to help you perfect these two.

Lost and Found

Time to add some color, texture, and density to your writing. Write with crayons or very thick markers and finish this story. **Start with:** *The moment I found that teeny, tiny ...*

TAKE THE NEXT STEP

Answer this teeny, tiny question: What is your writing goal? Answering this question every time you sit down to write (and the answers will vary from session to session) will keep you on a track to success.

OH NO

Use the expressions as you get to them. Start with: *"Oh No!" Why ...*

NO DICE

NO PROBLEM

NO TIME LIKE THE PRESENT

NO NEWS IS GOOD NEWS

NO SWEAT

NO WAY

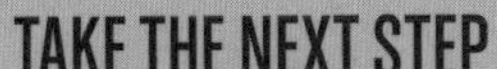

TAKE THE NEXT STEP

The next time you get a rejection or an unpleasant critique, don't think, "Oh no!" **Think the reverse: "On ho!"** Write how you'll handle this scenario to immediately move forward.

NAME GAME

Tell the origin of your first name. Were you named for someone? Is it a name of your parents' own creation? If you don't know the origin, make it up. You can also write interesting anecdotes about your last name. Be as wild as you like. Start with: *It was a difficult decision ...*

TAKE THE NEXT STEP

Choose a pen name, also called a *nom de plume*, for yourself. Does having one free you to write new topics? Why or why not? Do you feel like you want to save your best stuff for your own name?

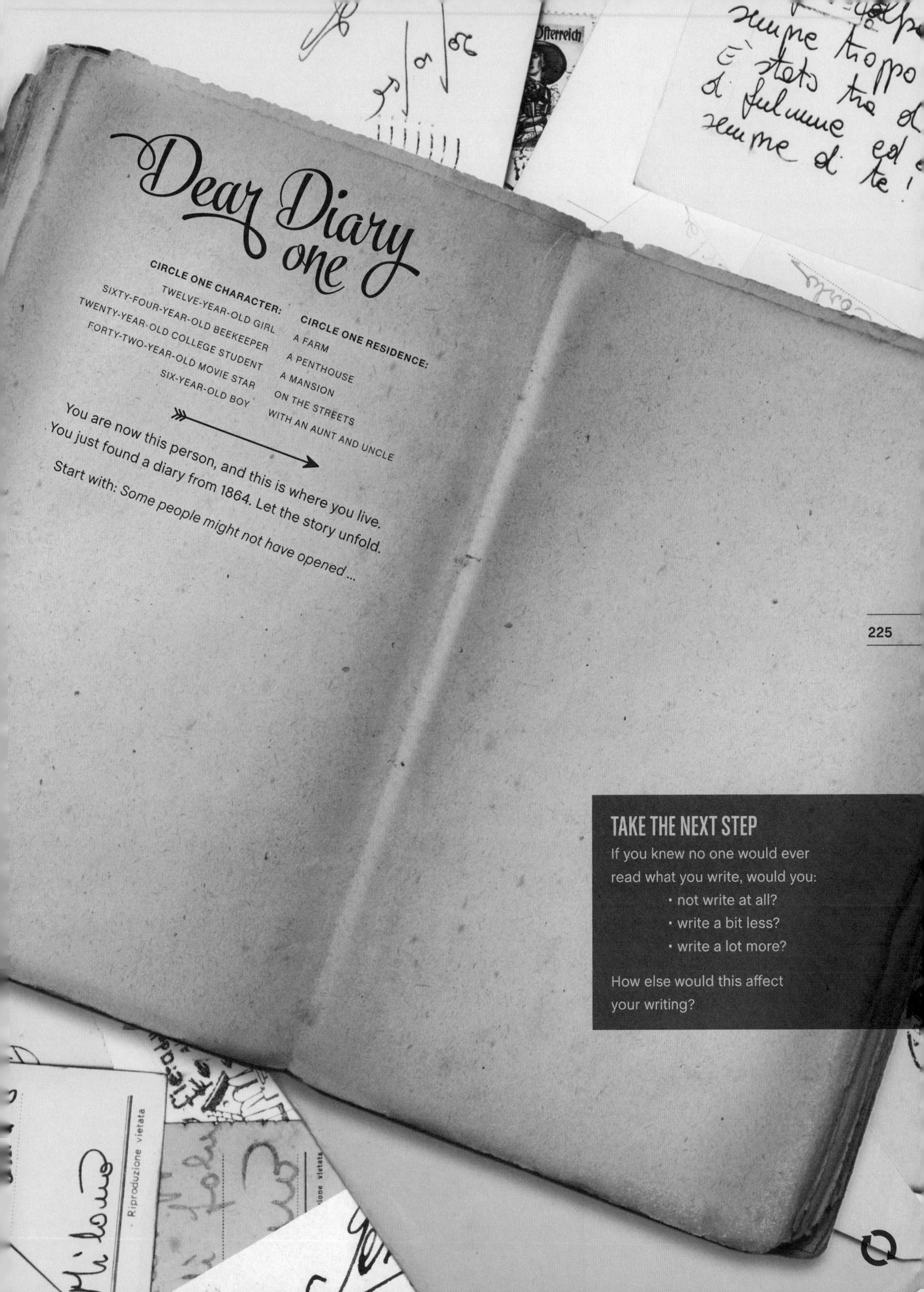

Dear Diary one

CIRCLE ONE CHARACTER:

TWELVE-YEAR-OLD GIRL
SIXTY-FOUR-YEAR-OLD BEEKEEPER
TWENTY-YEAR-OLD COLLEGE STUDENT
FORTY-TWO-YEAR-OLD MOVIE STAR
SIX-YEAR-OLD BOY

CIRCLE ONE RESIDENCE:

A FARM
A PENTHOUSE
A MANSION
ON THE STREETS
WITH AN AUNT AND UNCLE

You are now this person, and this is where you live. You just found a diary from 1864. Let the story unfold.

Start with: Some people might not have opened ...

TAKE THE NEXT STEP

If you knew no one would ever read what you write, would you:

- not write at all?
- write a bit less?
- write a lot more?

How else would this affect your writing?

the Green Room

Use the starting phrase and fill the page. *I was in one of my mint-green moods the day ...*

TAKE THE NEXT STEP

Whether you're in the green room or food shopping, as long as a scent is present, you can always practice writing. Write the first thing that comes to mind based on each of these aromas.

- Spearmint:
- Paint remover:
- Strong perfume:

IDIOMS DELIGHT · TWO

Start with the idiom *He always has a bone to pick ...*

Use the idiomatic expression *I haven't scratched the surface* in your conclusion.

TAKE THE NEXT STEP

Sometimes picking just one thing to write about feels like you're missing out on lots of other options. If you don't choose, however, you'll miss out on the joy of committing to, following through on, and completing something. Choose one writing project to commit to now. Keep a list of other topics for the future.

me times thirty-three

Use the word *me* thirty-three times in this piece. As you write each *me*, number it so you can keep track. The first *me* is provided for you! Start with: *She handed me the ...*

TAKE THE NEXT STEP

Speaking of you ... grade your writing work habits here (A through F).

[ ] completes projects on time
[ ] keeps a tidy area
[ ] asks for help
[ ] mentors others
[ ] keeps an eye on goals
[ ] is organized
[ ] is motivated to write
[ ] does paperwork
[ ] is inquisitive

DON'T SWEAT IT

Finish the story. Start with: *If I weren't allergic to sweating, I'd ...*

TAKE THE NEXT STEP

If you could plant one seed for your writing future, what would you want it to grow into? Do one thing today to nurture this seed.

GYMNASTICS

Use the given letter to begin each line of your story. Start with: *On my way to the gym ...*

G

Y

M

G

Y

M

G

Y

M

G

Y

M

G

Y

M

TAKE THE NEXT STEP

Olympic gymnasts have coaches who support them in their athletic pursuits. Writers can set up a writing-coaching partnership. You and your partner help each other stay on path for goals by asking questions. Here are some to get you started: What obstacle is keeping you from accomplishing ________________? Who put it there? Was it you? Can it be removed? How?

SPECTRUM

Each time you get to a color on the page, use it in your story. Start with: *The last time ...*

RED

BLUE

PURPLE

ORANGE

YELLOW

GREEN

TAKE THE NEXT STEP

Visualize enjoying your writing success: not one specific moment but rather what the full spectrum of day-to-day enjoyment will look and feel like. Visualize it daily so you are ready when the time comes.

Flipper one

Below are four backwards words. When you get to each word, flip it in your mind so it becomes a real word. Use that word in your story, before you get to the next word. (Don't read the words first—that spoils the fun!)

Start with: *I remember laughing ...*

DRIB

LIAN

KNIP

EPAC

TAKE THE NEXT STEP

A comedy-writing rule of thumb is to use lots of *K* sounds because they are naturally funnier than other sounds. Just saying *K* makes your mouth smile. Form a list of *K* words for future reference. Here's a start: *pickle, turkey, cucumber, Alka Seltzer ...*

SURE FOOTING

Finish these shorts. Starters are provided.

His feet look like Fred Flintstone's ...

One slip of the foot and ...

They say your feet don't burn when you do a fire walk ...

When his foot made contact with the ball ...

TAKE THE NEXT STEP

Until you put your foot down and actually set a goal—and go for it—you'll never know if you really wanted it in the first place. Nor will you find out what comes up for you that you might want instead. Create a writing goal. Go for it.

Gold Mold

Look around you. Notice all the *gold* things. Write down the first six you see:

1. __________ **4.** __________

2. __________ **5.** __________

3. __________ **6.** __________

Use all six in a piece. Start with: *Sometimes the dullest ...*

TAKE THE NEXT STEP

Even the dullest of writing days can be brightened with a laugh. Try this: Take off your shoes and socks. Put a pen or pencil between the two toes of your choice. Now sign your name. Don't be afraid to enjoy yourself ... or else it's time to get a new hobby!

twenty QUESTIONS one

Answer the twenty questions by circling one option. At the end you'll have a character sketch.

YOUNG or OLD?
THIN LIPS or THICK LIPS?
BLUE EYES or BROWN EYES?
ACTIVE or SEDENTARY?
EARLY BIRD or ALWAYS LATE?
TALL or SHORT?
MALE or FEMALE?
SOFT SPOKEN or LOUDMOUTHED?
BIG EARS or TINY EARS?
FAIR or DARK HAIRED?
NAIL BITER or WELL MANICURED?
GREEN THUMB or KILLS CACTI?
ORGANIZED or CHAOTIC?
SENSITIVE or CALLOUS?
THIN or FAT?
WIDE NOSE or SKI-SLOPE NOSE?
DOGS or CATS?
VANILLA or CHOCOLATE CAKE?
SMILING or GRIMACING?
HONEST or DISHONEST?

TAKE THE NEXT STEP

You have written a book titled *Bright Star*. Your publisher has just requested a brief bio for the back cover. Compose it.

You are this person. Write from his or her perspective. Start with: *The stars were so bright that night ...*

BROWN TOWN

Look around you. Notice all the *brown* things. Write down the first six you see:

1. __________
2. __________
3. __________
4. __________
5. __________
6. __________

Use all six. Start with: *I am usually oblivious to ...*

TAKE THE NEXT STEP

Very often we're oblivious to the multitude of sounds (or silences) around us. Take a moment now and simply listen. Then record all you hear. With this still echoing in your mind, work on incorporating sounds or hearing into your next writing

MAKING HEADLINES

You wake up one morning to the following newspaper story about you with the following title:

WRITER STRIKES IT BIG

What story does the article tell?

TAKE THE NEXT STEP

Practice your autograph so it reflects your writer personality: flowery, large, parochial, sloppy, neat, tight, all caps, etc.

FAMOUS FIRSTS

Finish the story.

Start with: *Happy families are all alike; every unhappy family is unhappy in its own way.*

THIS FIRST LINE IS FROM *ANNA KARENINA* BY LEO TOLSTOY.

TAKE THE NEXT STEP

Which one writer would you like to invite to a dinner party? What's the one question about writing practice or process you'd like to ask him or her? He or she has thrown this question back at you. What's your answer?

CONSTRUCTION WORKER COMMENTARIES

You are a construction worker. Complete each of these four short paragraphs in his voice.

Guns are ...

Stephen King is ...

The right to ...

Republicans are ...

TAKE THE NEXT STEP

Construction workers don't have the luxury of going back through their projects to redo what doesn't work. Fortunately, writers do. Even so, many writers fear the editing process. If you're one of them, take this opportunity to change your mind. Go back through these four writings and see how enjoyable it can be to strengthen your work by deleting all the unnecessary words.

Finish the story. Start with: *"What the heck am I supposed to do with this?" she ...*

TAKE THE NEXT STEP

"Do or do not. There is no try." —Yoda

Try to pick up this book. Notice that you are either picking it up or not picking it up—there is no middle ground. There is no such thing as try. Eliminate *try* from your vocabulary. Don't say, "I'm trying to write a screenplay." Say, "I am writing a screenplay." Hear how much better it sounds?

WHAT THE HECK?

Turkey Day

Finish the story. *What a turkey Uncle Ted was that day ...*

TAKE THE NEXT STEP

If you could achieve a writing dream by eating a two-inch cockroach, which dream would you do it for?

Cold Turkey

Finish the story. *She quit cold turkey and was actually doing quite well until ...*

TAKE THE NEXT STEP

Is there a time-wasting habit that you could quit cold turkey in order to gain ten minutes a day to write? Maybe one that has to do with e-mail, texting, or social media? Give it a try.

Sink Your Teeth into It

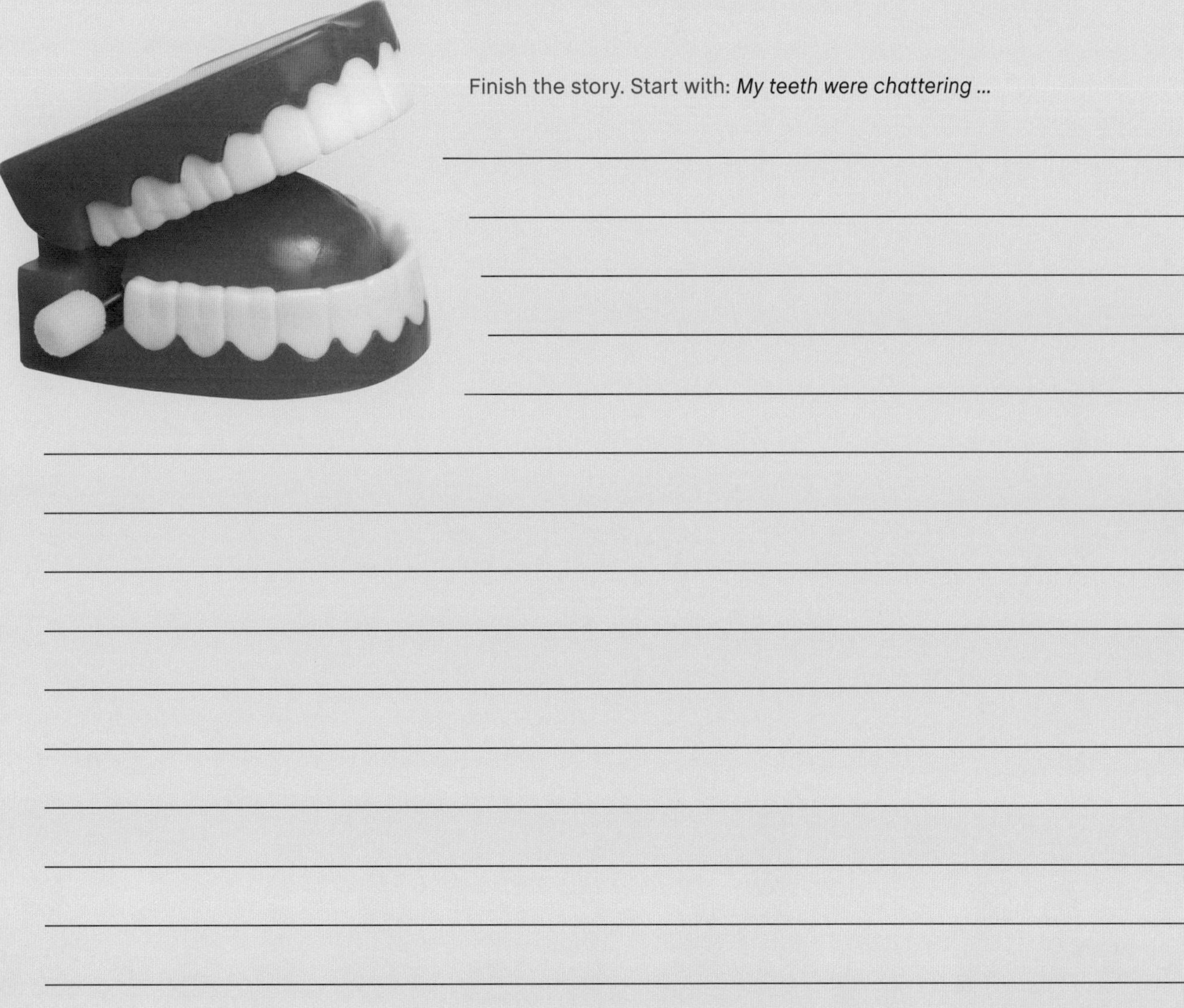

Finish the story. Start with: *My teeth were chattering ...*

TAKE THE NEXT STEP

Describe your current writing attitude as a type of food. Is it something you'd like to sink your teeth into? In your mind's eye, turn this attitude into a food you'd like to devour. My writing attitude was like a cold Pop Tart, and after I closed my eyes and concentrated I was able to transform it into an out-of-the-oven, thick, gooey pizza. Looks like I'm about to enjoy some yummy writing. I hope you'll join me.

JUNE THE JUNIPER

You are a groundskeeper who talks to all your plants. You believe that talking to them is better than talking to friends about your problems. One tree, a juniper whom you have named June, is your favorite. Start with: ***Can you believe it? She called me again last night ...***

TAKE THE NEXT STEP

Confide six memories that took place in your life in June. Use these to prompt further writing.

The year is 2525. You are a world-class bodybuilder, and you live in a town called Fishfoot. You just had a fight with your brother, named Slap, who is an air taxi driver. Your name is Stick. Start your story with: *Slap never understood my love of ...*

TAKE THE NEXT STEP

Here's an exercise to stretch your mental muscles. Describe how the word *slap* pertains to your writing. Now describe how the word *stick* does not pertain to your writing. Did you feel the mental burn as you stretched?

Bowl Me Over

To word-bowl, do your best to use each of the ten given words, one per line, in a ten-line story. Using them all equals a strike. Nine words on nine unique lines is a spare. Eight words on eight unique lines is a split. The words don't have to be used in the order given. Here's an example of a strike. The ten words are in orange.

1. I folded my **napkin**, placed it beside my plate, got in my car, and drove into the woods of
2. **Temptation** State Park. It's not exactly the best-named park since it has lost most of its
3. charm and allure from people tossing their trash, like **popcorn** bags and candy wrappers,
4. on the trails. I once organized an **Operation**-Park-Clean weekend, and many single-and-looking
5. people in a **variety** of ages, all 50+, showed up. Not much work got done since everyone was
6. too busy flirting and separating the **monsters** from the good prospects. One woman in a
7. way-too-tight **red** top actually began doing cartwheels to get attention when most of the
8. men were ogling a competitor who was dancing, actually **undulating**, with her hips moving
9. to the sound of some inner tone-deaf music. I guess my **quest** did return the park to a state
10. of "temptation" for the others. Disappointed, I drove off in my old **Saturn**!

Pick a set of ten word-bowling words.

1. collar, luggage, spoon, propeller, float, yogurt, trial, upper, version, worry
2. fork, socks, forward, airplane, devil, eloquent, gel, harvest, irate, junk
3. zebra, vest, kinship, lemon, mercury, nasty, overt, passion, rehearse, simple
4. molecule, mustard, murmur, pink, plum, pricey, quartz, quell, quiz, foreigner
5. bug, snow, banjo, schlep, burden, graduate, hamper, minister, cassette, perky

1. ____________________
2. ____________________
3. ____________________
4. ____________________
5. ____________________
6. ____________________
7. ____________________
8. ____________________
9. ____________________
10. ____________________

TAKE THE NEXT STEP

To extend your concentration, in addition to playing writing games like Bowl Me Over, it's also healthy to add some physical play to your creative life. Try skipping around the house, doing some jumping jacks, hopping in place on one foot, bouncing a ball against a wall, throwing a ball high in the air and catching it, jumping rope, or juggling. If you are embarrassed about your abilities, find a private spot to let your inner child play.

Early BIRD

Finish the story. *I was awakened at the crack of dawn ...*

TAKE THE NEXT STEP

Writing is like fishing. At dawn you go to a spot you believe is best, put bait on your line, and cast it. The flow, meditation, and predictability of the steps often lead to surprises. What is your writing bait? What surprises you about writing?

Write a fable about an ant and a worm. The moral of your story will be "Have courage."

Start with: *The worm crawled out of the hole ...*

WORM Hole

TAKE THE NEXT STEP

If you had the opportunity to travel through a wormhole, where in space-time would you like to exit? Jot down some notes so in the future you can write a story about this.

BODY TALK

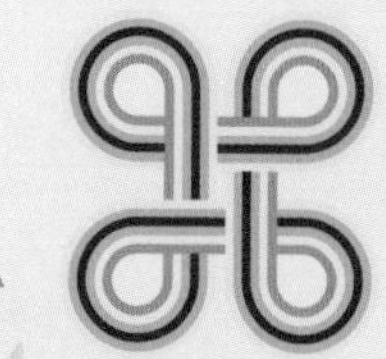

You just visited a psychic to find out what is in store for you. As soon as you leave the building, you grab your phone and call your best friend. Unfortunately, your call goes straight to voice mail. Leave a long message covering all the details, both good and bad. Use these nine words in your report:

deFEAT HANDy drIES gEARS besTOWS sTUNG NOSEy SHINdig NEEdle

Start with: *You'll never believe what the psychic said! The next time there is snow ...*

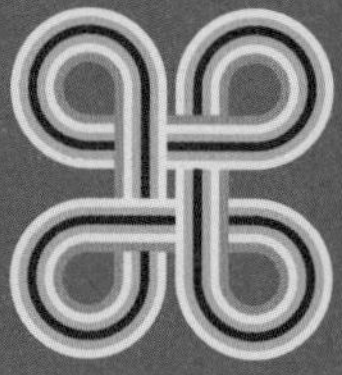

TAKE THE NEXT STEP

Listen and your ears will tell you what you don't hear as well as what you do hear. Have you ever heard the silence of snow? Try to capture the sound of sunshine in a sentence or two.

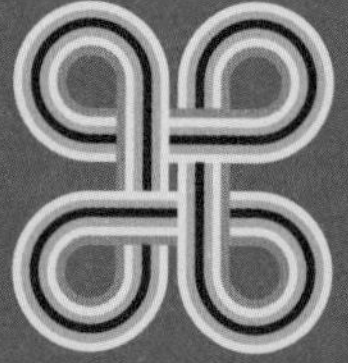

OH SO MAFIOSO

An excellent way to sound like the character you are portraying is to drop in some key slang terms. Here's your opportunity to let your imagination go for a ride as you write from the point of view of a mafioso (a member of a Mafia organization). Choose from this list of seventeen slang terms to make your character sound authentic:

CLIP: to murder; also *whack, hit, pop, burn, put a contract out.*

PINCHED: to get caught by the cops or federal agents.

JUICE: the interest paid to a loan shark for the loan.

CAPO: the Family member who leads a crew; short for *caporegime* or *capodecina.*

THE BOOKS: indicates membership in the Family. The books are open when there's a possibility for promotion.

POINTS: percent of income; cut.

SPRING CLEANING: cleaning up, hiding, or getting rid of evidence.

THE PROGRAM: the Witness Protection Program.

CONSIGLIERE: the Family advisor; the one who is always consulted before decisions are made.

EAT ALONE: to keep for one's self; to be greedy.

LARGE: a thousand dollars; also a *grand,* a G.

PAYING TRIBUTE: giving the boss a cut of the deal.

WASTE MANAGEMENT BUSINESS: euphemism for organized crime.

SOLDIER: the bottom-level member of an organized crime Family, as in "foot soldiers."

FUHGEDDABOUDIT: stands for "Forget about it."

FRIEND OF OURS: how one member informs another that a new acquaintance is also a member (*used in the starter*).

CODE OF SILENCE: not ratting on a colleague once he has been pinched.

Start with: *Before things got complicated, the only thing I knew about Anthony was that my uncle introduced him as a "Friend of Ours."*

TAKE THE NEXT STEP

At some point, unfortunately, someone is probably going to negatively critique your creative endeavors—intentionally or by accident. Instead of letting it hurt and discourage you, do your best to *fuhgeddaboudit*. It's about the person doing the critiquing; it's *nodaboutchew*. To deflect it, immediately shift into tough-guy mode and, in your best Brooklyn accent, silently chant *fuhgeddaboudit* over and over to yourself until you can let it go and *laughaboudit*. Then get back to following your passion.

Make Believe

Finish the story. Start with: *I used to pretend ...*

TAKE THE NEXT STEP

Pretend you are an archaeologist digging up feelings from when you were three years old. What do you find? How can you incorporate these feelings into your current writing?

Finish the story. Start with: *He took one look and whistled a long and drawn out "Beeeee-uuuuu-teeeee-ful ...*

TAKE THE NEXT STEP

From *The Book of Qualities* by J. Ruth Gendler: "Beauty is startling. She wears a gold shawl in the summer and sells seven kinds of honey at the flea market. She is young and old at once ..." Personify your writing practice.

One-Liners

In this story, use as many of these Henny Youngman one-liners as you possibly can (or possibly can stand!):

Answers are what we have for other people's problems.

A Sunday picnic with the kids is no picnic.

To a bald man dandruff is a thrill.

Home is where the mortgage is.

A little gossip goes a long way.

He who laughs, lasts.

Take my wife, please.

Start with: *The place was a real dump ...*

TAKE THE NEXT STEP

If your mental state is as overloaded as a dump, it's hard to write. List things you need to clear from your mind to make more room for writing.

Your mind is now clear. Start writing!

Where Have You Been?

Use these four words:

yellow

iris

quote

joke

Start with: *"Where have you been?" she demanded. He dropped his eyes and ...*

TAKE THE NEXT STEP

Do you drop your eyes when people ask about your current writing? Practice so you can answer with confidence next time—while looking the asker in the eye.

BIG CHEESE

Write in and around the pictures and holes on the page as you choose.
Start with: *He was the most pompous ...*

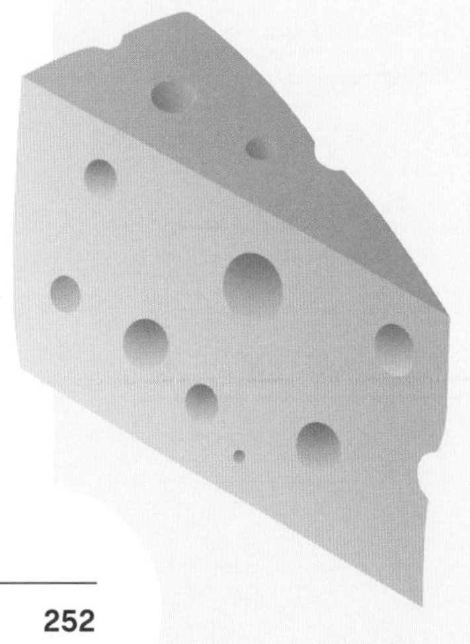

TAKE THE NEXT STEP

The more cheese ages, the better it is. The younger a vegetable is, the better it tastes. What about your current age enables you to be a better writer?

WHAT A CHARACTER! * ONE

Pick an age between two and eighty-eight: ________

Select an eye color: ________

Choose a hair color: ________

Write the name of a city or town: ________

List a type of residence: ________

Write a first name starting with *G*: ________

Write a last name starting with *S*: ________

Describe a prominent physical feature: ________

____

Reveal a quirk or mannerism: ________

____

____

You are now officially this character. Start with: ***I remember when the power went off ...***

TAKE THE NEXT STEP

Don't worry if you feel an oncoming creativity power outage. This is a vital part of the creative cycle, called the "receptive phase." When you're in this phase, it's important to relax and let ideas and inspirations flow through you. Something will spark the next part of the cycle, called the "active phase." It's important to learn to enjoy both parts of the cycle. To practice, go out into the world and receive!

Finish the story. Start with: *The worst snowstorm was in the winter ...*

TAKE THE NEXT STEP

One way to develop your powers of observation is to avoid listening to the "experts." For example, without first listening to a forecast, go outside and observe the sky, the horizon, and the current weather. Describe it, and perhaps even create your own forecast. Then listen to the meteorologist. See how unique (or perhaps accurate) your descriptions and forecasts are.

Finish the story.

I refuse to accept money for shoveling Mrs. Walker's driveway and sidewalk, but I would never turn down a cup of her hot cocoa. Today, after she shared the secret to her recipe, I broke down and told her the secret of what's happening in our ...

TAKE THE NEXT STEP

Is there some stage of writing about which you are pulling a snow job—a deception—on yourself? For example: You are ready to complete (or submit) a piece of writing but keep convincing yourself it is not ready. Change this mind-set before it snowballs into reality.

Kleptomania

Find a book or magazine, and steal the first line to begin your piece on this page. If you don't have a book or magazine handy, use this starter: *He hopped off the horse like a Hollywood cowboy ...*

TAKE THE NEXT STEP

Stealing (well, borrowing) from the lives of others is what writers do. List three details you've read or heard about others that would work well in a story. Combine them all into a story you write in the next ten minutes. Set a timer now!

LABYRINTHINE

Life offers many twists and turns, and a theory exists that many of them come to the surface when you walk a labyrinth from the entrance into the center and then back out the exact same path. Here's a slight twist on that idea. You are going to write your way in and then back out of the same path of the labyrinth below. If you write small enough you will be able to see what you've written both ways. But it's more liberating to write large on the way in and write just as large and right on top of your words on the way out. Something about the impermanence and illegibility of it all frees you to write whatever you feel and prevents you from worrying about the end result. Give it a try. A starter has been provided for you. Just follow the path in and back out again.

TAKE THE NEXT STEP

As you were writing, were you surprised by how long it took to write your way through the labyrinth? Did you stick with it? Did you quit? How did it feel when you finally exited again? Amazing how a labyrinth is a microcosm of the writing process. The next time you write, remember to be patient and take it one step—or word—at a time. Don't get frustrated in the middle. You *will* finish, and you *will* come out the other end ... and most likely you'll be happier and filled with a sense of accomplishment. If you ever come across a life-size labyrinth, try walking it. It's a neat experience.

Selfie

We've all taken selfies. But have you ever written one? Using words, describe a selfie moment you wish you had captured with a photo. Your only restriction is that you may only write on the screen to the right. A starter has been provided.

TAKE THE NEXT STEP

In 2013 the word *selfie* was named "word of the year" by the *Oxford English Dictionary*. To qualify for such a title, words must reflect "the ethos, mood, or preoccupations of that particular year." What do you do to stay on top of publishing trends, writing news, and, most important of all, the interests of the audience for which you typically write?

CHIP OFF THE OLD BLOCK

You are an alien who has been sent to Earth. You arrive in the heart of New York City and land in the middle of a city block. The first thing you encounter is an unidentifiable object (known to Earthlings as a melting chocolate chip.) Study it. Send a transmission back to your planet about your first Earthly discovery!

Start with: *We have met our first ...*

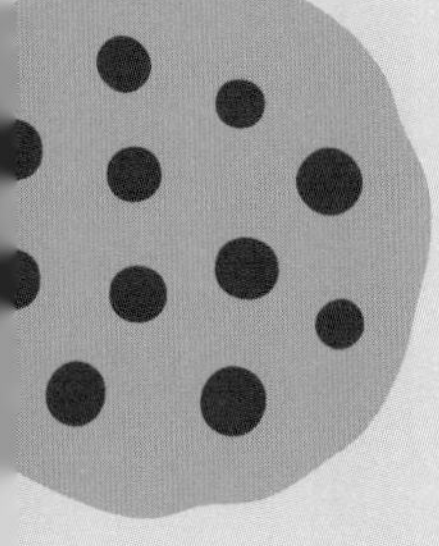

TAKE THE NEXT STEP

Describe your writer-self in terms of being a chip. Are you a chocolate chip, a potato chip, an ice chip, or some other chip? Why? What can you do to make your chip more chipper? Try it!

Dance Lessons

Finish this sentence, and then use it in your story.

It's exactly like____________________________________,
which is how I feel about going to the ballet.

Start with: *Sometimes it takes more than once for me to learn a lesson ...*

TAKE THE NEXT STEP

When writing, you and your pen are dancing on paper. Describe an experience in which the pen took the lead and you merely followed. (Make one up, if necessary.)

DANGER US

Finish the story. Start with: *That was, by far, the most dangerous thing I've ever ...*

TAKE THE NEXT STEP

Sometimes we don't write for fear there will be (dangerous) repercussions from what we put on paper. Nowhere in the definition of writing does it say we must share with others. Write what you want. But first (right now), hug yourself by wrapping your arms around your body while reminding yourself that you are safe. Go ahead—do it. It feels good!

WEIRD WORDS · TWO

Use the words *cedi, ekpwele, kwacha*, and *ouguiya* in your story—even though you probably don't know what they mean. Set your story in New York City at the height of a summer heat wave. Start with: *The layers of ...*

(These words are international currency. *Cedi* is used in Ghana, *ekpwele* is used in Equatorial Guinea, *kwacha* is used in Zambia, and *ouguiya* is used in Mauritania.)

TAKE THE NEXT STEP

We all overuse words. My husband complains that I use *awesome* to describe everything from a new sponge to professional fireworks. We also underuse words. For example, how easy is it to refer to yourself as a writer, an author, a poet, a blogger, a publisher, or a journalist? Time to start adding these awesome (I couldn't resist!) words of self-description to your vocabulary.

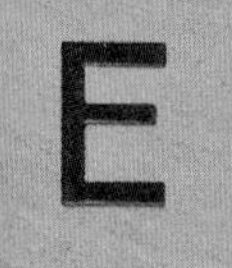

MADE-UP WORDS · ONE

Connect these prefixes, roots, and suffixes as you like to come up with four made-up words:

PREFIX	ROOT	SUFFIX	YOUR MADE-UP WORD
mal	money	licious	1.
free	pure	ment	2.
bi	layer	ling	3.
non	tree	ism	4.

Use all four in this story. Start with: *I get such a kick out of ...*

TAKE THE NEXT STEP

When you link money with writing practice, does it give you an extra motivational kick? Or does it have the opposite effect? Why?

Finish the story. Start with: *Now I recall, that was the day I overslept ...*

TAKE THE NEXT STEP

What writing task could you accomplish if you set your alarm fifteen minutes earlier just for tomorrow? Do it. What could you accomplish if you did this the day after tomorrow, too?

Bubble Rap * Two

Create a dialogue between two people, using the speech bubbles provided. The blue bubbles are for one person, and the green bubbles are for another person.

TAKE THE NEXT STEP

We can rap about what we plan to do until we're blue in the face. Our actions, and, in particular, the consistency of our actions, are what matter. In what area of your life do you show consistency? How can you transfer this to your writing practice?

Truth Is Stranger Than Fiction

Write an autobiography of a phase of your life. Make sure everything is true except one detail, which is 100 percent made up. Read it to your friends, and see if they can pick out the lie! Start with: *When I was ...*

TAKE THE NEXT STEP

Write down two lies you tell yourself about not being good enough.

1. ______

2. ______

Now take a thick black marker and cross out the lies until they are no longer part of your internal repertoire. Feel better?

CONSTRUCTION PHRASE

Select one word from each column, and write them all below. This will construct a six-word phrase for you to start this writing assignment.

COLUMN 1	COLUMN 2	COLUMN 3	COLUMN 4	COLUMN 5	COLUMN 6
The	haiku master(s)	sadly	deface(d)	fences	by
A	lion tamer(s)	angrily	describe(d)	newspapers	with
Many	martial arts teacher(s)	adamantly	deliver(ed)	hiccups	along
Some	money lender(s)	anxiously	demand(ed)	monkeys	that
Few	missionary(s)	eagerly	delegate(d)	pies	to
No	alien(s)	rudely	detain(ed)	children	or
Three	accordion player(s)	randomly	debate(d)	pharmaceuticals	because
When	cashier(s)	boisterously	document(ed)	books	from
Before	dog walker(s)	calmly	destroy(ed)	candy	and
Ninety-nine	rollerblader(s)	perfectly	double(d)	cookies	after

Your picks:

TAKE THE NEXT STEP

Success is constructed on failures: Paul Newman auditioned for a very minor role in a high school play but failed to get the part. Jerry Seinfeld had a recurring role in a TV sitcom but was fired after three episodes. Meredith Vieira was let go from a local TV station in the 1970s. These people, who are practically superheroes in their chosen fields, could have quit after being rejected, but they didn't. If you love writing, you should stick with it.

Pick a Little, Write a Little

Pick one of the "quantity" choices from the first column, and write it on the first line below the box. Do the same for the adjective, noun, and past-tense verb columns. When you're finished, you will have created an odd starting phrase. Now circle a word from the last column—you must include it in your writing. Pick a time limit that suits your current schedule, set a timer, and write until the time is up.

QUANTITY	ADJECTIVE	NOUN	PAST-TENSE VERB	CIRCLE A WORD TO INCLUDE:
Too many	miserable	security guards	cried	ballroom
Six hundred	euphoric	laptops	rolled	dimple
A few	contagious	cameras	chewed	ebony
A tad less than a million	fragile	dragons	entertained	globe
Fewer than a dozen	bouncy	magicians	fought	hammer
Forty-two	determined	militia	jumped	lemon
A dozen or so	grumpy	marshmallows	rotated	mermaid
Scores of	inquisitive	criminals	drew	pelican
An unknown quantity of	jealous	goldfish	strolled	rain
Massive quantities of	bedraggled	football players	ate	underwear
Hardly any	pushy	spirits	materialized	violin
A small majority of	slow	wizards	caught	yo-yo

Write your picks here:

TAKE THE NEXT STEP

When making choices, most people fall into two major categories: Satisficers and Maximizers. Satisficers take action once their criteria are met. As soon as they find the car that has the qualities they want, they are satisfied and make a decision. Maximizers want to make the optimal decision. Even when they find the car that meets their requirements, they can't decide until they explore every available option. In his book *The Paradox of Choice*, Barry Schwartz argues that Satisficers tend to be happier than Maximizers. Where do you fall on the spectrum? How about when it comes to choosing writing projects to work on? And what about when you're deciding when a written piece is complete or not?

FAR, FAR AWAY

Think of a person who really bugs or annoys you. Think of a place you'd like to send this person. Then—mentally—send them there! With that in mind, start with: *The postcard arrived ...*

TAKE THE NEXT STEP

Describe the ideal place to write. Be very specific and detailed.

Go there in your mind the next time you write. See how your writing changes.

Footsies

Finish the story. Start with: *Painted toenails always ...*

TAKE THE NEXT STEP

If the soles of your feet had eyes that could see through floors and earth, what would they see right now? Write it.

Writing practice combines your power of observation and your power of imagination.

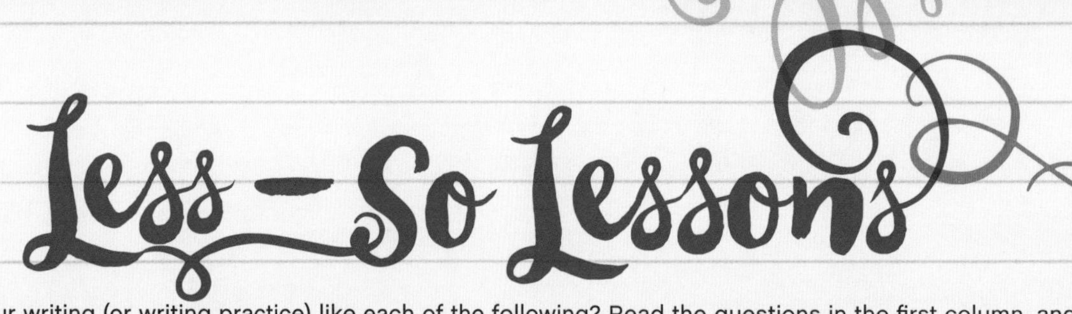

Less—So Lessons

How is your writing (or writing practice) like each of the following? Read the questions in the first column, and then answer briefly in the second column. Note in Column 3 whether this approach is troublesome for you or a good thing. Move to Column 4, and jot down one idea to make the troublesome ones less so and the good ones more so. When you have completed all ten questions, pick one and put it into action today.

HOW IS YOUR WRITING LIKE ...	ANSWER BRIEFLY HERE:	IS THIS TROUBLESOME, OR IS THIS A GOOD THING?	JOT DOWN ONE IDEA TO MAKE IT LESS SO OR MORE SO:
Being on a diet?			
Sailing?			
Going on a first date?			
Conducting an orchestra?			
Riding a roller coaster?			
Cooking a gourmet meal?			
Planting a vegetable garden?			
Disciplining a toddler?			
Organizing a revolution?			
Building a house?			

TAKE THE NEXT STEP

On my car I have a magnet that reads: PURR MORE—HISS LESS. If you had a similar magnet about your writing, what would it read?

__________________ MORE— __________________ LESS

CRAVEN LION

See how many words—of four letters or more—you can make from the letters in the word *craven*, which means cowardly. Aim for fifteen words. (A full list appears at the bottom of this exercise.) List them here.

Try to use all fifteen words in a story that begins: *I was craving ...*

(carve, crave, rave, raven, cave, cavern, vane, cane, aver, crane, care, race, acre, earn, near)

TAKE THE NEXT STEP

Both cowardly feelings and obsessive cravings appear in our nighttime dreams. Keeping a dream journal provides good fodder for writers. Take a minute right now to record a recent dream to use as a spark for a future writing.

LIONHEARTED BY DAY

Finish the story. Start with: *Her name was Kimba, and I ...*

TAKE THE NEXT STEP

Are you most creative in the morning, afternoon, evening, or night? What about this time of day helps you be creative? What can you do to mimic this prime-time-of-day setup to enjoy similar writing conditions during other times of the day? Try it.

Bald Ballerina

Start with the word *bald*, and free-associate. Write down whatever comes to mind.

Bald

Circle six interesting words from your writing above. Use them in a story whose main character is a ballerina. Start with: *I was backstage ...*

TAKE THE NEXT STEP

Think of a project you've put on the back burner. List the pros and cons to completing it. Whether you choose to finish it or to let it go, you'll feel better knowing you made a choice.

Petite Paragraphs 3

Here is a chance to write short paragraphs of memory snippets. Use the starters provided.

I remember rushing ...

I remember pulling ...

I remember pushing ...

I remember covering ...

I remember deciding ...

I remember choosing ...

TAKE THE NEXT STEP

Remember what it feels like to be relaxed? Tense every muscle in your body at once and hold for twenty to twenty-five seconds. Release and shake it all out. Aaah. Now write.

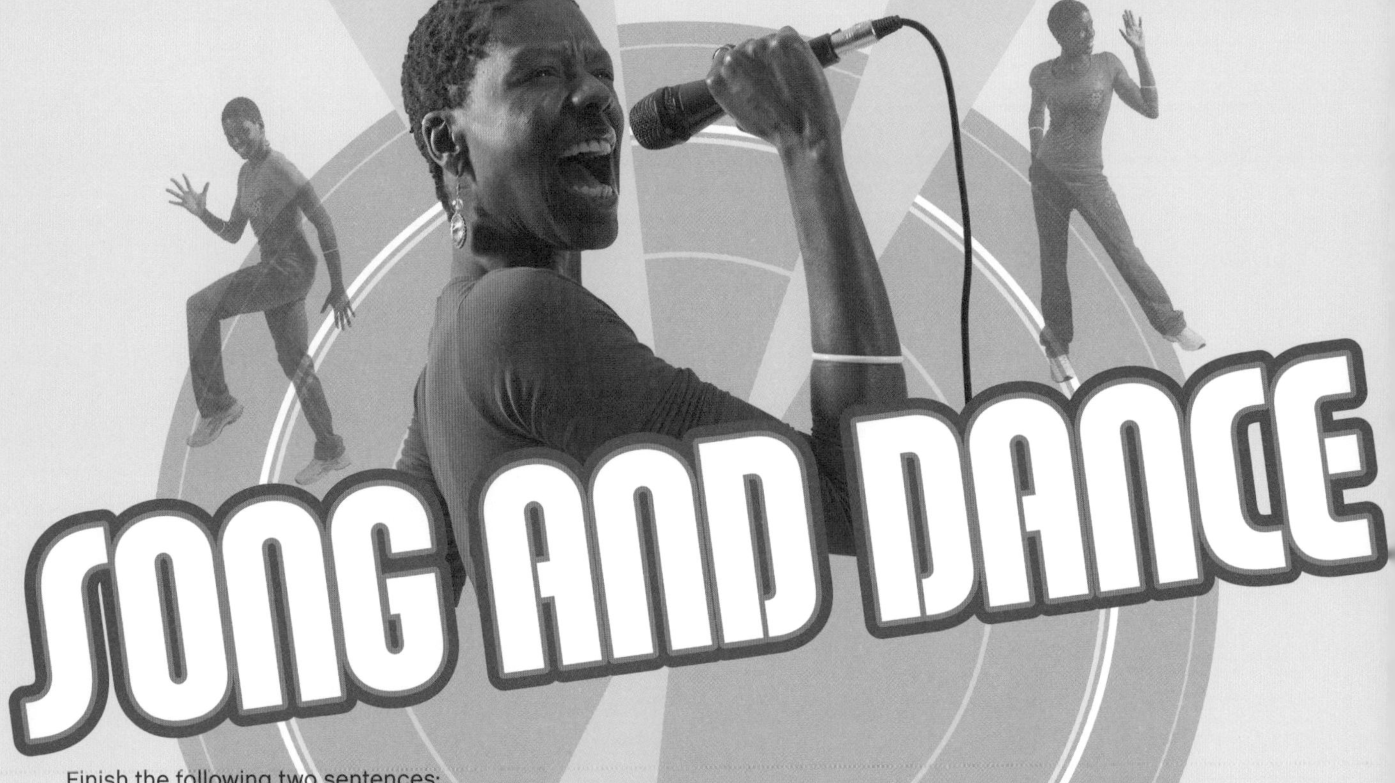

Finish the following two sentences:

My singing voice sounds like ...

When I dance I look like ...

Now use these two full sentences in a story that starts with: *We made a left onto Canal Street ...*

TAKE THE NEXT STEP

Compare writing to singing or dancing. How is writing different? How is writing easier? How is writing harder? How are they similar? How can you combine all three?

TRUE (OR FALSE) CONFESSIONS

You are on a long-distance bus ride. Even though you got on at the same terminal as the person sitting next to you, you are positive you have never seen him or her before, and you are equally certain you will never see this person again. You plan to not share your name or any other information that would enable this person to identify you. Then, feeling confident that your secret will remain safe, you choose to confess something to this person.

Pick something from this list, and make it pivotal to your confession: Counterfeit, Chamber, Chinatown, Cheated, Chain, Boyfriend, Bullet, Bungled, Brown bag, Bribe, Misunderstood, Money, Murder, Memory, Master plan, Vase, Vestibule, Vehicle, Violent, Vault, Fog, Fraud, Homicide, Husband, Hunting, Hurt, Papers, Permission, Pickle, Prohibited, Lawyer, Lost, Loot, Lifted, Love, Shop, Smuggle, Stalk, Stranger, Sin, Accident, Arson, Arrest, Afterthought, Anxious

Start with: *A while back ...*

TAKE THE NEXT STEP

Confessing a fear or doubt you have about you as a writer will help you begin the process of overcoming it. Write your confession on a piece of paper, and then read it aloud to yourself. Now write down the opposite of this confession or a related statement that casts you in a positive light. Cross out the original confession. Look in a mirror, and read the new, opposite statement aloud. Do this again and again until you have memorized it and can look yourself in the eye while saying it. Example: *Because I never studied English or grammar, I feel like a fraud when someone asks me to proofread their writing.* Rewrite: *When I proofread someone's writing I have a talent for hearing (inside my head) the grammar mistakes in order to make the necessary corrections.* Big difference, eh?

Use one of these superstitions to inspire your next writing:

- If a bee enters your home, it's a sign that you will soon have a visitor. If you kill the bee, the visitor will be unpleasant.
- Touch blue, and your wish will come true.
- If your right ear itches, someone is speaking well of you.

Start with: *Whenever the phone rings ...*

TAKE THE NEXT STEP

You pick up the ringing phone, and a (living) writer you admire is on the other end. What would you say to get him or her to agree to read something you've written? Put these words in a note, find the writer's contact info, send the note, and then forget about it.

WHAT A COINCIDENCE

Life is full of coincidences. Write about one that you actually experienced. Start with: *What a coincidence ...*

TAKE THE NEXT STEP

It's not a coincidence that ideas come when we're shopping. Describe a character based solely on these cart contents: orange flip-flops, a dead-bolt lock replacement kit, and a twelve-pack of yellow legal pads.

The next time you shop, check out others' carts and allow your imagination to create more characters or writing exercises based on the contents.

What a Character! TWO

Circle an age:

18 19 20 21 22 23 24 25 26 27 28

Write an eye color:

Jot down a hair color:

Record the name of a city or town:

Pick a type of residence or a house:

Choose a prominent physical feature:

List a passion:

Create a name using the initials *C* and *B*:

You are now officially this character. Start with: *I thought I had been asking politely, but obviously ...*

TAKE THE NEXT STEP

Dialogue is a great way to start a story. Imagine two airport baggage claim attendants are your characters. Set a ten-minute timer, and let the characters talk.

Waiting in Line

Start writing down the first column, fill it up, and then write down Column 2 ... and so on until you get to the end of the sixth column.

Start with:
Waiting for ...

1

2

3

4

5

6

TAKE THE NEXT STEP

If you were waiting in line at a book signing for your favorite author, what would you tell people who aren't in line about this author's writing that might make them want to join you? Now think about what you hope others will say about your writing when they talk about it. Keep working towards this.

Initial  Initials

Use your first and last initials to generate the components that will make up this story.

	BEGINNING WITH YOUR FIRST INITIAL	BEGINNING WITH YOUR LAST INITIAL
Body of water		
Flower		
Food		
First name (other than your own)		
Last name (other than your own)		

You now have two characters—one from each column—and a bunch of words to use creatively! For example: If your flower is *petunia*, use it as a nickname. If your food is *Fruit Loops*, use it for someone's state of mind! If your water is *babbling brook*, use it in a metaphor.

Write about these two characters, starting with: *Sometimes things just ...*

TAKE THE NEXT STEP

Think about the initial spark that made you want to start writing. Now that you've re-captured it, what can you do to keep that spark alive every time you sit down to write?

Dear Diary 2

CIRCLE ONE CHARACTER OPTION:

- ninety-nine-year-old woman
- thirty-six-year-old bartender
- seventeen-year-old high school football player
- fifty-five-year-old divorced man
- forty-three-year-old astrologer
- eight-year-old girl

CIRCLE ONE RESIDENCE OPTION:

- Brussels, Belgium
- on the bayou
- on a college campus
- a hotel
- on the grounds of a resort
- an old lighthouse

You are now this person, and this is where you live. You just found a diary from 1492. Let the story unfold. Start with: *I expected to find ...*

TAKE THE NEXT STEP

Columbus sailed the ocean blue in 1492. If you had lived in his time, would you have been an explorer? In what areas of your writing could you be more adventurous? Pick one and explore it today.

BATHROOM HUMOR

When I lead writing workshops, we go around the circle and introduce ourselves with a few words. Introductions are almost never about writing. Some examples are: a favorite Halloween costume, what you eat for breakfast, or how many times you reset the snooze setting on your alarm clock. The most humorous of all topics was sparked by a most untidy restroom in the bookstore where we were meeting: "Describe your favorite public restroom ... and if you don't have one, describe your least favorite." Time for you to do the same ... now!

TAKE THE NEXT STEP

Take this book with you into the bathroom, and stand in the shower or tub. Shout, "I am a writer!" five times. Let it echo off the walls.

Describe a memory from your past that this moment triggers. Do this in other places in your home, and then write the memories.

At-EEEEEEEEEEE-tude

Finish the story. Start with: *Born on the wrong side of the tracks, she was a tough ...*

TAKE THE NEXT STEP

With whom do you feel most comfortable being your writer-self? Why?

With whom do you feel most uncomfortable being your writer-self? Why?

Do something to change this.

Think about a banana ... the feel, smell, taste, and color. Write three memories or impressions that come to mind.

1. ______

2. ______

3. ______

Now use these three in a story. Start with: *It was really nice ...*

TAKE THE NEXT STEP

If the phrase "Nice guys finish last" is true, which of your "nice guy" traits can you eliminate to get further ahead in your writing? With this trait gone, what will you do today to move your writing along?

NARROW ESCAPE

Sometimes the width between the lines on the page influences what you are writing. Try this one with very narrow spaces. Start with: *Escaping was the only ...*

TAKE THE NEXT STEP

Write about a place where you can escape to (even if it's only in your mind's eye) when things get rough. Use all five senses so someone else can actually see, feel, hear, taste, and smell it.

SCRIBBLE TWO

This exercise uses letter tiles like those found in a familiar word-based board game. When you get to a letter and use it as the first letter of a word, you get two points. Try for one hundred points!

YOUR SCORE: ________

Being in limbo ... A R A

I A

R R

O Y

H G

V E Q

E N M M

I O

E

E O U A

R X

A U L

L T B I

B U O

A C E

T A

C

E E

A I K

Y F

TAKE THE NEXT STEP

In 100 words or fewer, describe a time when you felt extremely alive. Use this feeling when you write next.

Hate to Love

With a series of one-letter changes, the word *hate* turns into *love*.

hate rate rave cave cove love

Use all six of these words in this piece. Start with: *The Eskimos ...*

TAKE THE NEXT STEP

Your writing is thrilled that you are giving it so much time and attention. It's so thrilled, it is now writing you a love note. Lend it your pen and your hand, too, so the message is legible.

VERY TOUCHING

Think of a slinky. Write four textures that come to mind.

1. ______________ 3. ______________

2. ______________ 4. ______________

Now think of a scarf. Write four textures that come to mind.

1. ______________ 3. ______________

2. ______________ 4. ______________

Use all these in a story that begins: *Late-night city streets were the perfect backdrop for ...*

TAKE THE NEXT STEP

What's the ideal motivational backdrop to hang behind you when you write?

Find or take a picture, or draw or make a collage, that ignites this mood. Hang it behind you. When you need a bit of motivation, take a mini-vacation and turn around to look at it.

SENSORY OVERLOAD

Write down the following:

Something you see at an executive conference:

A clothing texture you like:

A smell from the city:

A sound associated with a farm:

A taste reminiscent of your childhood:

Use all five items in your writing. Start with: *The cathedral bell ...*

TAKE THE NEXT STEP

Every July 4, the Liberty Bell is symbolically rung. (It's too cracked to really strike.) Whenever I want to congratulate myself but my situation restricts me from doing so, I make a fist with my left hand and lift it quickly upward once. No one notices, and I feel great. What physical gesture can you come up with to silently acknowledge yourself?

WHAT A CHARACTER!

3

Pick an age between forty-eight and ninety-eight:

Hair color:

Eye color:

Name of a city or town:

Type of residence or house:

Last name starting with *S*:

First name starting with *R*:

Pet peeve:

Favorite place to go:

You are now OFFICIALLY this character. Start with: ***The meteor …***

TAKE THE NEXT STEP

Mobiles that hang over babies' cribs don't usually have meteors on them. But often they do have stars, moons, suns, and other objects to gently stimulate the baby. What six stimulating things would you put on a mobile to hang over your writing area? Perhaps you should make one.

Pick a color you like. Write it (or one of its shades) inside each bracketed space on the page. Now fill in the rest.

Start with: [ ] *like a ...*

[ ]

[ ]

[ ]

[ ]

[ ]

[ ]

[ ]

TAKE THE NEXT STEP

When you are deep in the flow of writing, what color crayon or marker are you? Why? To jump-start your flow, or to keep the momentum of your writing going, get a marker or crayon in this color. Write with it tomorrow—all day!

SHAPE UP

Use these four shorts to get in shape. Use the shapes provided as part of your creation. Write between the shapes as well! If you like, try to connect all your short pieces with a common theme.

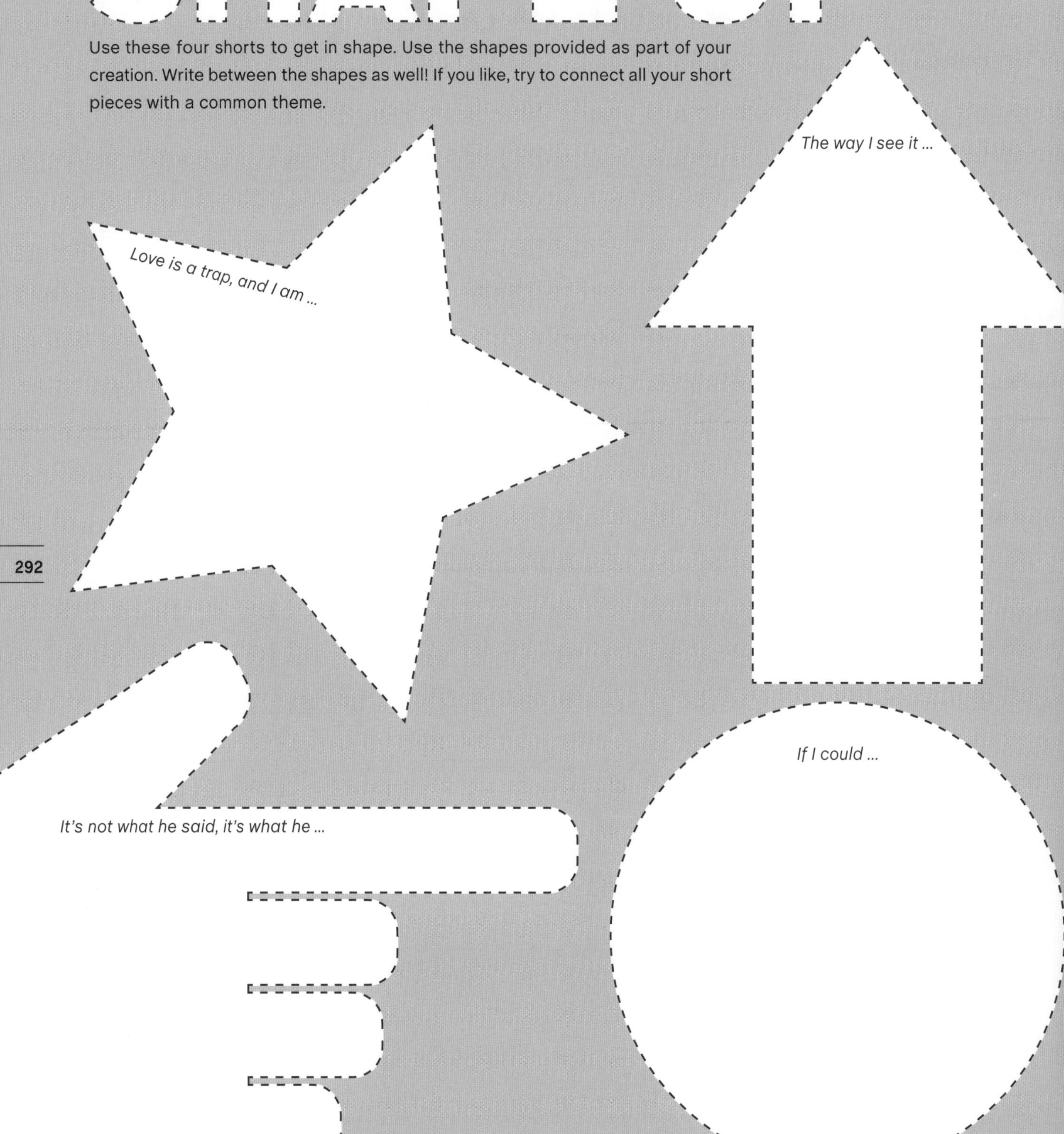

TAKE THE NEXT STEP

Combine getting in shape with writing by doing a cardiovascular exercise before you write. While your heart's still pounding hard and you're still sweating, put pen to paper. Before you try it, how do you think this will affect your writing?

VISIONARY

Finish these shorts. Starters are provided.

He winked at me ...

I blinked and ...

She batted her eyes ...

He was always squinting ...

TAKE THE NEXT STEP

Visionaries see trends. Writers must also track trends in order to submit timely articles and book proposals. List three trends you now see from reading, observation, contact with youth, etc. that you would like to write about. Tackle one!

Weird Words 3

Use the words ***EDDA***, ***IDUN***, ***ATLI***, and ***EGIL*** in your story—even though you probably don't know what they mean. Set your story during the gold rush.

Start with: *The rope was tight ...*

(All are Norse words: *Edda* means "prose," *idun* means "mythological woman," *atli* means "mythological king," and *egil* means "mythological hero.")

TAKE THE NEXT STEP

Ever notice how you learn a new word and suddenly it's everywhere? The same holds true for thoughts. Focus on something positive you want in your writing life. Write it down. Now see how it appears and what happens.

NAMING NAMES TWO

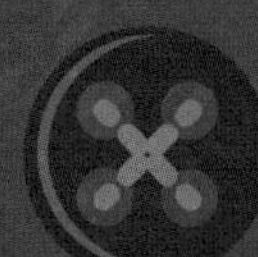

Finish all four of these shorts. The starter will stay constant, but your name will change.

Your name is *ASHLEY*. Start with: *The plaid shirt ...* ______________________

Your name is *FANNY*. Start with: *The plaid shirt ...* ______________________

Your name is *TAB*. Start with: *The plaid shirt ...* ______________________

Your name is *MAURICE*. Start with: *The plaid shirt ...* ______________________

TAKE THE NEXT STEP

If you were to name your writer-self, and the first three letters of each name had to be *PRO*, would you be PROfessor PROcrastinator PROmetheus? PROlific PROfit? PROcessor? Or another? Be a PROfessional writer, and give yourself a first, middle, and last name all beginning with the letters *PRO*.

Jewel • Eye • Fourth

Incorporate an eye, a jewel, and the word *fourth* in this story. Start with: *July in the city is usually a time when …*

TAKE THE NEXT STEP

List six memory jewels that took place in a July of your past. Use these to prompt further writings.

News-y Twos-y

Walter Cronkite always signed off his newscast with the line "And that's the way it is."
Use this quote two times in this writing exercise. Start with: *He worked up a good lather ...*

TAKE THE NEXT STEP

Jot down four stories you've heard or seen in the news that would make good starting points for stories, blogs, or articles. The next time you need something to write, use one of these.

Pick Six • One

Without moving, write down six things within your line of vision: they can be actions, people, items, textures, or emotions:

Now use all six of these things in a piece that begins: *It's funny, the more I ...*

TAKE THE NEXT STEP

Point of view influences a story. Go back and change the POV in your writing above from first person (*I, we*) to third person (*he, she, it, they*). Do you think you'll only change pronouns? What other changes do you expect to make? Now do it. What surprised you?

SIGNS OF THE TIMES

Use the traffic sign words as you come to them.

Start with: *Every time I ...*

SOFT SHOULDER

YIELD

MERGE

SLOW

TAKE THE NEXT STEP

Do you have an idea of how much time you spend writing (not only creatively) every day? Keep a twenty-four-hour log to see. Include texting, e-mail, making lists, etc. Before you do it, guess how much time you think it amounts to. When done, come back and see how close you were.

IDIOMS DELIGHT 3

Start with the idiom *I can't put my finger on it, but ...*

Use the idiomatic expression *Head and shoulders above the rest* in your conclusion.

TAKE THE NEXT STEP

Who was head and shoulders above the rest in terms of encouraging your creativity? Even if he or she only encouraged you a teeny bit, write a two-line thank-you to him or her.

no ifs, ands, or don'ts

Don't use any of these words in your story:

cold	ice	winter
chill	sleet	freezing
snow	flurry	shiver

Start with: *We arrived in the Arctic at noon and immediately ventured out into the thirty feet of blinding white ...*

TAKE THE NEXT STEP

Fill in the blanks.

If I had ________________________, then I'd write ________________________.

If ________________________ didn't matter, I'd write ________________________.

If I was guaranteed ________________________, I'd write ________________________.

Assume one of these statements is true for the next twenty-four hours. Now write your heart out.

Walk the Line

Write on the continuous line all the way to the end, rotating the book as you go.

Start with: *What started out as a casual walk ...*

TAKE THE NEXT STEP

Think of the very last person you saw or spoke to. If you were to "walk in their shoes," what would the new you write about? Can you turn one of these ideas into a project?

SHADOW FIGURES

Use the words as you get to them. Start with: *Shadows don't usually scare me ...*

marshmallow

mango

milk

mud

mothballs

mink

TAKE THE NEXT STEP

If writing is putting words on paper one after another the way walking is putting one foot in front of the other ... then what are the shadows that make writing scarier?

SOUNDS LIKE...

B C D G J K L O P R T U X Y

Use all the above letters as initials, letters, or as the words and names they also sound like.

Start with: *We were in alphabetical order ...*

TAKE THE NEXT STEP

Sometimes the alphabet isn't sufficient to make a point. Many artists sign their paintings with a symbol. Create one to reflect your writer-self. If you can draw stick figures, you can do this!

In Pennsylvania, most license plates are three letters and four numbers, such as BMN 1958. For this exercise use the three letters as the first letters of the three beginning words in your story. Example: *Because most nice ...* Use the four-digit number, 1958, somewhere in your story. Example: *A study says that nice people are 1,958 times more likely to say yes.*

Start here:

B M N

TAKE THE NEXT STEP

Being too nice (taking on too much or trying to be perfect, for example) may backfire and turn into self-sabotage. Be nice to yourself now, and write all the things you want from others and from yourself that will help your writing. Then tell or ask someone for what you want. Doing so is very freeing.

FOR WHOM THE BELL TOLLS

Finish the story. Start with: *The factory bell ...*

TAKE THE NEXT STEP

A bell rings to signal the end of the workday. If you had all the freedom in the world, how would you spend your free evening? Go there in your mind. Writing is a great escape that takes you places you wouldn't otherwise go for an evening.

ALPHA-BRAVO-CHARLIE

Finish this story using the NATO Phonetic Alphabet chart to the right. Your starter: *I managed to shout into the mouthpiece, "ECHO-NOVEMBER-ECHO-MIKE-YANKEE----SIERRA-PAPA-OSCAR-TANGO-TANGO-ECHO-DELTA" before ...*

A	Alpha
B	Bravo
C	Charlie
D	Delta
E	Echo
F	Foxtrot
G	Golf
H	Hotel
I	India
J	Juliet
K	Kilo
L	Lima
M	Mike
N	November
O	Oscar
P	Papa
Q	Quebec
R	Romeo
S	Sierra
T	Tango
U	Uniform
V	Victor
W	Whiskey
X	X-ray
Y	Yankee
Z	Zulu

TAKE THE NEXT STEP

Your "India-November-November-Echo-Romeo----Charlie-Romeo-India-Tango-India-Charlie" is definitely your "Whiskey-Oscar-Romeo-Sierra-Tango----Echo-November-Echo-Mike-Yankee." Using the NATO Phonetic Alphabet, write what it would feel like to send your critic as far away as possible with a one-way ticket.

COACH

Think of a sports coach or gym teacher you've known. Use this person as a springboard, yet feel free to embellish and be inventive with the following attributes.

Physical body type: ______________________________

Style of walking: ______________________________

Usually wears: ______________________________

Prominent facial feature: ______________________________

Reaction under stress: ______________________________

Nonsports passion: ______________________________

You are now this person. Start with: *The clock was ticking, time was running out ...*

TAKE THE NEXT STEP

You can't always control the timing of deadlines or overlapping commitments—but you can control how you handle yourself. Write a mantra to repeat over and over the next time time isn't on your side. Commit it to memory so when your next deadline looms, you'll be okay.

OnoMaTopoeiA

Onomatopoetic words imitate sounds associated with the objects or actions they refer to. Here is a long list. Feel free to add more of your own!

hiss, ping, crunch, pop, sizzle, bang, swish, smash, flutter, clunk, peck, whistle, smack, whack, hush, whir, tiptoe, whoosh, thud, zap, twang, cock-a-doodle-doo, squish, stomp, tap, thump, splash, purr, tinkle, gush, kerplunk, slurp, swirl, crash, whirl, clang, mumble, squeak, boom, meow, plop, cuckoo, pow, splat, quack, screech, zoom, ticktock, burp, clip-clop, eek, hiccup, moo, oink, buzz

Now, using the first line of Edgar Allan Poe's short story "The Tell-Tale Heart," write your own story incorporating as many of these words as possible.

True! Nervous, very, very dreadfully nervous I had been and I am: but why will you say that I am mad?

TAKE THE NEXT STEP

Another example of a writing practice that can be done anywhere is to simply listen to what's going on around you. Write the first thing that comes to mind from these sounds.

- Ticking: ______
- Grinding teeth: ______
- Popped balloon: ______
- Rain on metal: ______

Happy Endings • Three

Use the last sentence at the bottom of the page to conclude your story.

He never saw her again, nor did he ever discover whether she had told him a lie or was speaking the truth.

(The last sentence is from *A Meeting* by Guy de Maupassant.)

TAKE THE NEXT STEP

Go back through this book to make sure you weren't lying when you wanted to be laying.

INFINITIVE	to lay	to lie
PRESENT	lay(s)	lie(s)
PAST	laid	lay
PAST PARTICIPLE	laid	lain
PRESENT PARTICIPLE	laying	lying

To *lay* means "to put or place something down." To *lie* means "to rest or recline."

TARGET PRACTICE

When you write, try to hit your target audience. Choose a target audience for this writing: kids, tweens, teens, young adults, men, women, or seniors. Now write specifically to them using the starter provided.

My aim is usually better ...

TAKE THE NEXT STEP

Make a list of things you aim to write about in the future. Write each on a slip of paper (like a fortune cookie fortune), and put them in a jar. If you're ever wandering aimlessly in the land of writing, pull one out and use it to give yourself direction.

MADE-UP WORDS · TWO

Connect these prefixes, roots, and suffixes in whatever combination you wish in order to generate four made-up words.

PREFIX	ROOT	SUFFIX	MADE-UP WORD
re	splitter	ing	1.
pre	pepper	izer	2.
un	mimic	athon	3.
dis	photo	ator	4.

Use two of your made-up words in a story. Start with: *He tried to make himself invisible ...*

TAKE THE NEXT STEP

Combine these jumbled prefixes, roots, and suffixes to create a word that positively describes your writing process.

pro, super, sym, comp, form, styl, spin, tale, flow, mus, word, izer, ing, ator, aptor

Hang it on your wall, and look at it often!

313

TAKE THE NEXT STEP

The next time you pick up this book, let go of the intensity and smile—a big ear-to-ear grin. Keep it on your face while you write. What do you expect will happen to your writing? Tomorrow, check back and see if your prediction was right or wrong.

Underdressed and Under Duress

Free-associate with this string of words. Fill this space, letting one word trigger the next: **soda, bubbles, belch**

Now pick three words from your list and use them in a story.
The title of your story is: "Underdressed and Under Duress."

TAKE THE NEXT STEP

When you write in this book, are you usually under a state of duress? What is it that truly motivates you and gets you to put words on paper? (Dig beyond the obvious answer.)

Think of this tomorrow when you write.

PETITE PARAGRAPHS • FOUR

Here is a chance to write short paragraphs of memory snippets. Use the starters provided.

I remember tormenting ...

I remember walking ...

I remember diving ...

I remember begging ...

I remember bragging ...

I remember dividing ...

TAKE THE NEXT STEP

When in need of a quick writing exercise, you can always start with *I remember*, *I want*, *I seem*, or *I feel*. Come up with some other short starters to use in the future.

HOME AWAY FROM HOME

Draw a big tree on this page. Imagine yourself on the grass (good thing I provided that part for you!) leaning against the tree. Complete the following two prompts.

I SMELL: ______________________________

____

I HEAR: ______________________________

____

Now draw a tree house in your tree. Imagine climbing up into it. (Either draw a ladder or give yourself magical powers!) Now envision yourself inside. This is your very own writing studio. Since it's in your mind, you can make it as large as you like. Go ahead and mentally decorate it by adding some stuff that makes you happy. Now take a seat (quick—add seating if you need to) and picture yourself relaxing in your home away from home. It's time to answer the following:

I SEE: ______________________________

____

I FEEL: ______________________________

____

BEING HERE MAKES ME WANT TO WRITE ABOUT: ______________________________

____

____

____

Now start writing it! Yup. Right here. Write now.

TAKE THE NEXT STEP

Draw what your face looks like when you imagine yourself in your tree house, uninterrupted and feeling creative: If you practice visualizing and carrying your tree house with you in your mind and heart, your face could look like this no matter where you are. Give it a try.

NOCTURNAL

Finish the story. Start with: *He haunted the night like a ...*

TAKE THE NEXT STEP

Haunted houses make great settings for stories. List locations you know firsthand that would be good for stories, books, articles, etc. Pick one, and get started now.

Rhyme Time

Write two nouns that rhyme: ____________________ ____________________

Write two verbs that rhyme: ____________________ ____________________

Write two adjectives that rhyme: ____________________ ____________________

Write two names that rhyme: ____________________ ____________________

Write a story using all eight words, starting with: *When I asked ...*

TAKE THE NEXT STEP

If a genie appeared, what three writing wishes would you make? The criteria for listing them is that they must all rhyme somehow. Do something now toward making one of them come true.

Three Wishes

Fill the page. Start with: *He wished he ...*

TAKE THE NEXT STEP

My mother-in-law (whom I never met) was known to say, "Wish in one hand, poop in the other. See which you get first." Take an action today to turn a wish into a reality. Write down the wish. Write what action you will take to make it happen. Now do it!

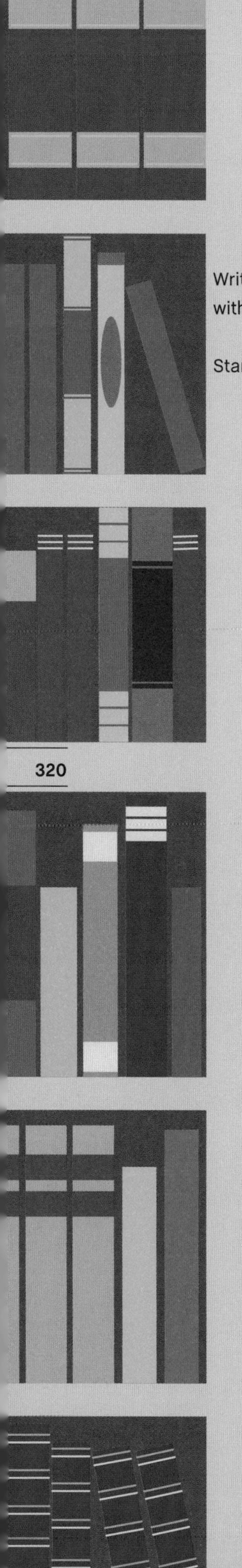

FICTIONARY TWO

Write a dictionary-style definition for the word *indaba* (pronounced "in-DAH-ba"). Use *indaba* with your fictitious definition in a story.

Start with: *The scream was loud ...*

(The definition of *indaba*: a conference of indigenous peoples of Southern Africa.)

TAKE THE NEXT STEP

If you were to arrange a conference of mentors, whom would you invite? What's one question you would ask them all? Answer it yourself now.

X MARKS THE SPOT

Begin with the supplied starter, and then write anywhere and everywhere on the page, inside and outside the *X*. Use the spots as you get to them. They can be part of a drawing you use to illustrate your story, bullet holes, or simply periods. Let your imagination guide you!

My ex-

TAKE THE NEXT STEP

If you were to closely **EX**amine the **EX**pectations you have for yourself as a writer, would you say they propel you forward or stop you in your tracks—or somewhere in the middle? **EX**plain.

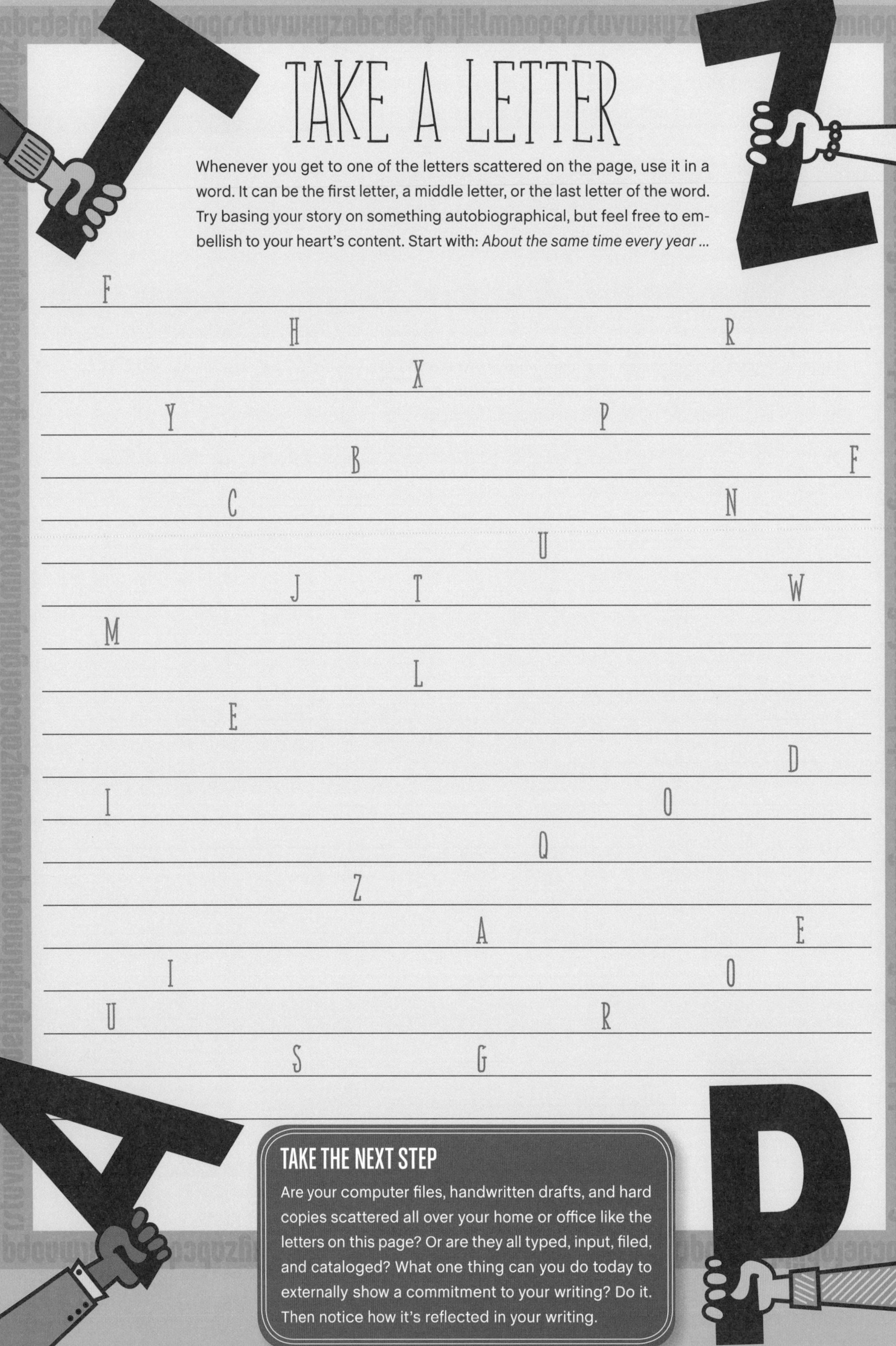

TAKE A LETTER

Whenever you get to one of the letters scattered on the page, use it in a word. It can be the first letter, a middle letter, or the last letter of the word. Try basing your story on something autobiographical, but feel free to embellish to your heart's content. Start with: *About the same time every year ...*

TAKE THE NEXT STEP

Are your computer files, handwritten drafts, and hard copies scattered all over your home or office like the letters on this page? Or are they all typed, input, filed, and cataloged? What one thing can you do today to externally show a commitment to your writing? Do it. Then notice how it's reflected in your writing.

Can You Believe it?

Finish these four short shorts. Starters are provided.

I can't believe I was afraid of ...

I can't believe I was intimidated by ...

I can't believe she never told me ...

I can't believe how many years it's been since ...

TAKE THE NEXT STEP

Sometimes it's hard to remember all the things we accomplish. Take a few minutes now to record the non-writing things you have accomplished since starting this book. No item is too small to qualify for the list, but please don't list things you always do. Working hard in one area often spills into others. Keep up the momentum!

FATHER AND SON

You are a father who just discovered a major dent in your car. You approach your teenage son.

Start with: *It has come to my attention ...*

TAKE THE NEXT STEP

A great way to brainstorm a story is to start with questions such as:

What would life be like if ________________________?

What would happen if ___________________________?

Fill in these blanks, and then actually answer one of the questions you just created.

SNAPSHOTS TWO

"Word Snapshots" are a way for writers to capture photo-like images by using only words. Try to capture colors, textures, and expressions as you use the following starters. Use your own life story ... or make it up!

A city vacation ...

Children playing ...

Dancing ...

A war ...

TAKE THE NEXT STEP

List six snapshots from your life that took place in May. Use these to prompt further writings.

PHILATELY WILL GET YOU NOWHERE

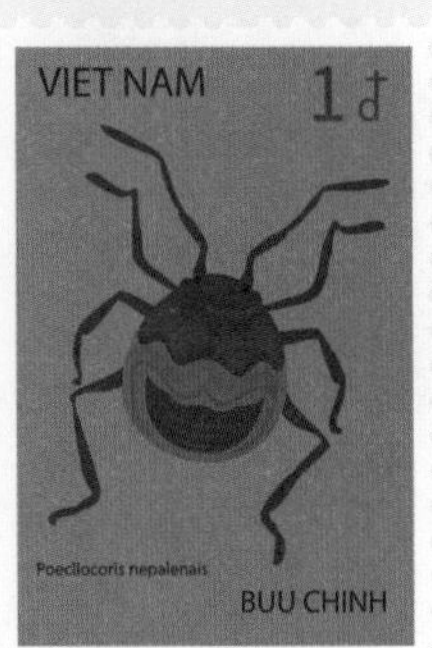

You are a devout stamp collector. You meet the person of your dreams and make a date. Unlike your date, you are as nice as can be. Tell the story. Start with: *I wish I could turn back the hands of time ...*

Use the line "Philately will get you nowhere" in your conclusion.

TAKE THE NEXT STEP

If you approached your writing the way a devoted philatelist tends to his stamp collection, what would you do differently? Try this approach the next time you write, and see what's different!

MY CONDIMENTS TO THE CHEF!

mayonnaise
mustard
pickle
ketchup
hot peppers
relish
soy sauce

Use all of these words in a piece that starts: *His taste in music was...*

TAKE THE NEXT STEP

To make Russian dressing, mix ketchup, mayo, and relish. Can you think of three pieces of unfinished writing you could combine to come up with one new, completed work?

GREEN WITH ENVY

Describe your favorite green thing in great detail:

Now circle five of the most intriguing words from this description and use them in a story. Start with: *The leprechauns brought me ...*

TAKE THE NEXT STEP

In presentation, both color and lack of color make an impact. Experiment with this by getting a pencil and blackening in an area on a blank piece of paper. Now write with the eraser.

Ved-dy In-ter-es-tink!

Think of an accent or dialect you like. Write using that accent. Spell the words the way they sound when pronounced. If you were writing with a German accent, *think* would be written *tink*, and *what* would be *vhat*. If it's a Boston accent, *park* would be *pahk*, and *car* would be *cah*.

Start with: *The moment I arrived ...*

TAKE THE NEXT STEP

Think about words you like because they make you feel good. Perhaps it's their sound, an odd spelling, a connotation to something in your life, or their pure power. Jot them down and use them. They just might have the same effect on your readers.

I didn't know ...

Upside down

Turning things over doesn't only have to happen in your mind! For this exercise, try a new perspective by turning the book upside down. Use the starter provided.

TAKE THE NEXT STEP

If you don't know what success looks like or feels like, then how will you recognize or enjoy it when it happens? (It may be happening right now!) Write what success feels or looks like for you.

REFRIGERATOR COMMUNICATOR

PART ONE: Use the starter on the fridge, and write until you fill the refrigerator on the page. When you get to each magnet, make sure you write only one word inside it. When you are done, look at the directions for Part Two. No peeking!

PART TWO: Write all the words you wrote inside the magnets on the lines below. Then look at the directions for Part Three. No peeking!

PART THREE: Using the twenty words from Part Two, create a poem. Then hang it on your fridge for all to read.

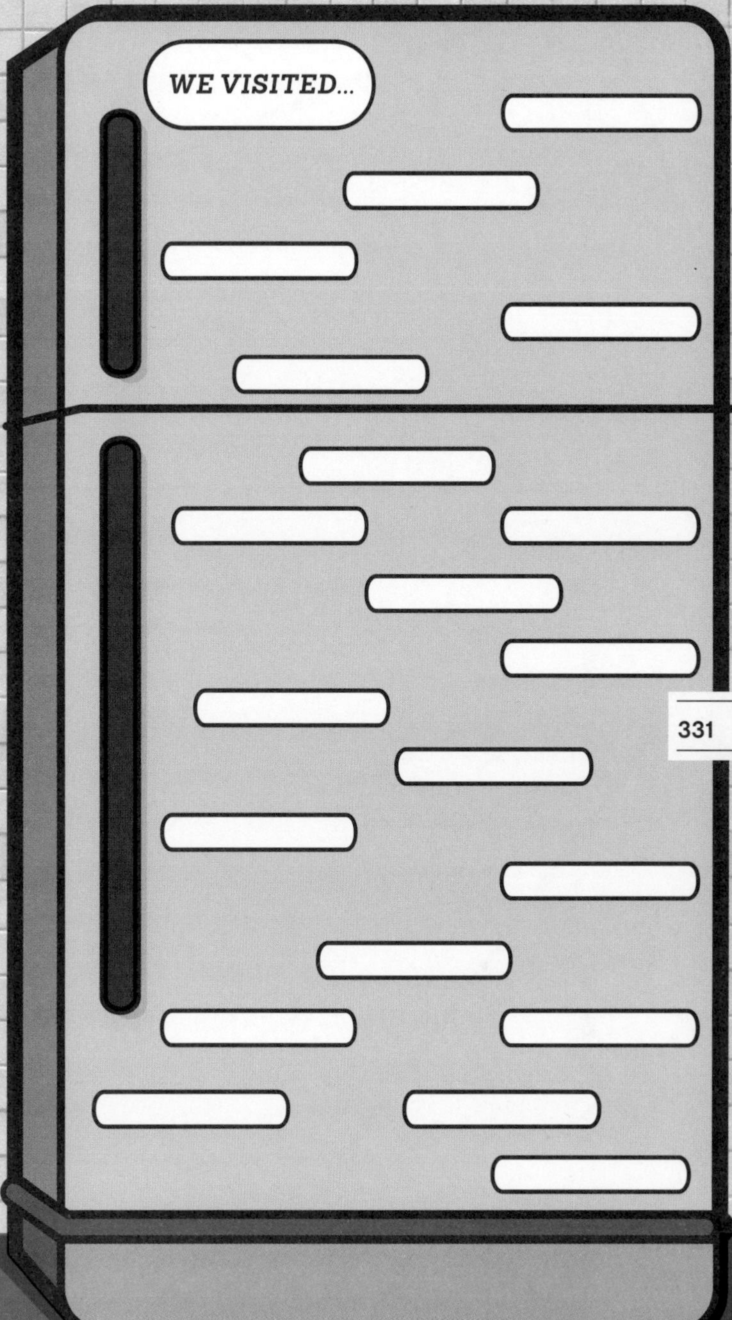

TAKE THE NEXT STEP

Want to do this again? Copy this page, and cut out all the magnet areas. Place the page on top of something you've written, or a newspaper article, print book, or e-book. Copy all the words that appear in the holes. (You may have to manipulate the template a bit in order to view a full word within each magnet area.) Then turn those words into a poem. Flip over your template for another selection. It's also fun to make templates that have some larger spaces to capture phrases.

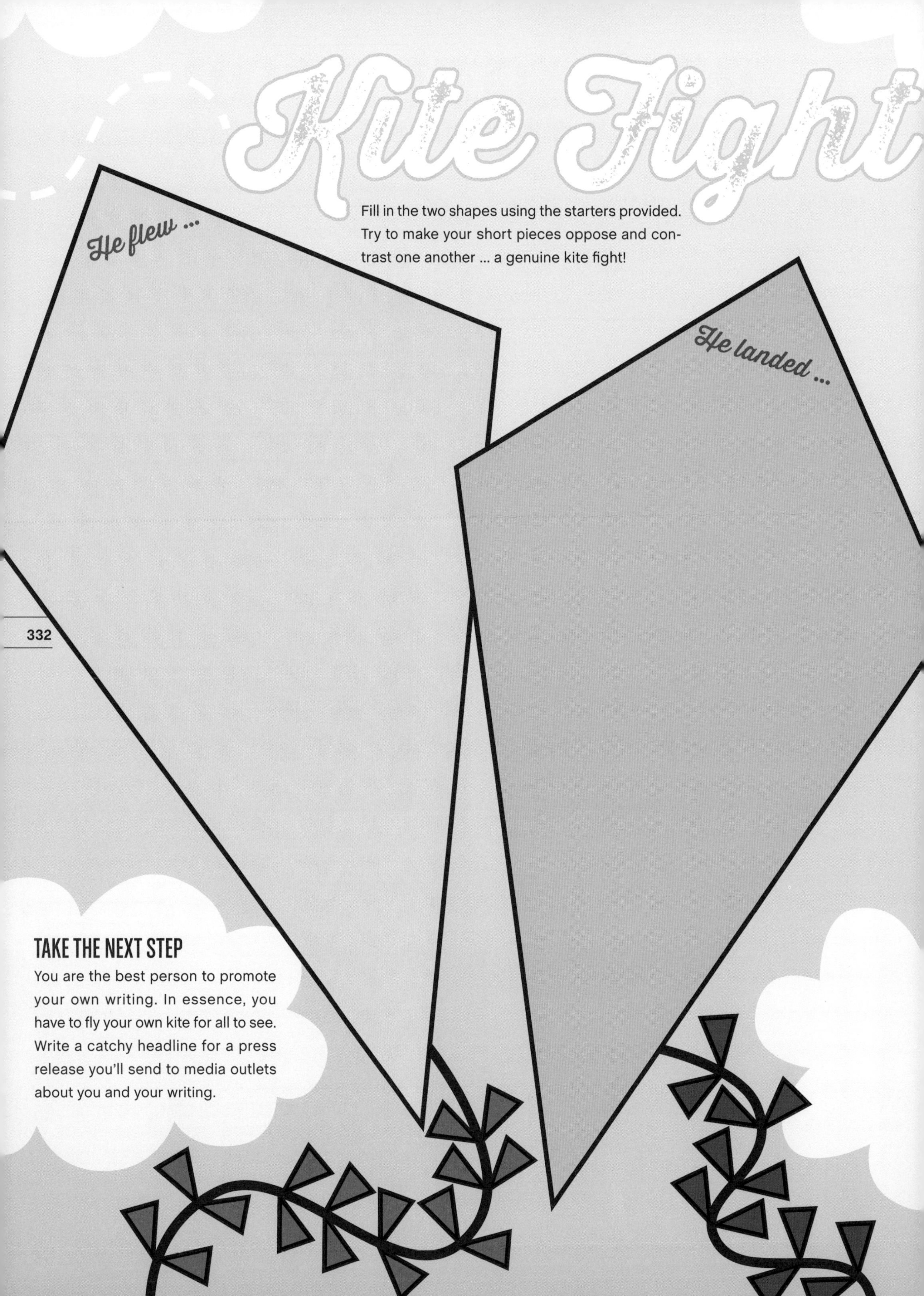

Kite Fight

Fill in the two shapes using the starters provided. Try to make your short pieces oppose and contrast one another ... a genuine kite fight!

He flew ...

He landed ...

TAKE THE NEXT STEP

You are the best person to promote your own writing. In essence, you have to fly your own kite for all to see. Write a catchy headline for a press release you'll send to media outlets about you and your writing.

"QUOTE, UNQUOTE"

"I hate writing, I love having written." —DOROTHY PARKER

Use the quote above somewhere in your piece. Start with: *I hate the texture of ...*

TAKE THE NEXT STEP

Search through books or on the Internet for a quote that motivates you to write. Copy it here and also on a piece of paper.

Carry it with you until you've committed it to memory. Then pass the paper to someone else who would benefit from this wisdom. Ask him to memorize it and to pass it on to someone else.

REUNION

These twins appeared in a dream you had two nights ago about a fifty-year high school reunion. This was strange because it's only been five years since you left high school. This evening at the supermarket, oddly enough, you ran into one of them, and he addressed you by name. Finish the story. Start with: *"Hello Wanda. Did you enjoy ...*

TAKE THE NEXT STEP

What about writing do you enjoy?

What about writing gives you satisfaction?

PICK*SIX*2

Without moving, write down one thing within your line of vision: an action, a person, an item, a texture, an emotion, etc. Then repeat this until you have a total of six things.

1st Thing: ____

2nd Thing: ____

3rd Thing: ____

4th Thing: ____

5th Thing ____

6th Thing: ____

Now use all six of these in a piece that begins: *From out of the blue ...*

TAKE THE NEXT STEP

It's tough on your muse if you always force her to appear from out of the blue. Make it easier by creating a ritual around your writing time and place. Perhaps light a candle at the beginning of the session and extinguish it at the end. Devise a ritual that works for you.

FAMOUS FIRSTS ✧ THREE

Finish the story. Start with: *One day back there in the good old days when I was nine and the world was full of every imaginable kind of magnificence, and life was still a delightful and mysterious dream, my cousin Mourad, who was considered crazy by everybody who knew him except me, came to my house at four in the morning and woke me up by tapping on the window of my room.*

(This first line is from *My Name Is Aram* by William Saroyan.)

TAKE THE NEXT STEP

What excites you about beginning a project? What scares you about it? List ideas on how you can turn this fear into excitement every time.

No, No Barrette

Finish the story. Start with: *Back then we all wore our hair ...*

TAKE THE NEXT STEP

Often my hair resembles a garden in need of weeding. If your writing practice were a garden, what would you weed out? What would you plant?

SBIL DAM·TWO

Just like Sbil Dam—One, this is Mad Libs—just in reverse. Instead of filling in the blanks with random words, you will write the story that goes around those words. First fill in truthful answers on the lines above all the clues in parentheses. Then use the starter provided to begin writing. Whenever you get to the info you filled in, incorporate it into the story. Remember: You don't need to use the words as they were originally intended. For example, if a game you enjoy is Monopoly, that word could also be used to describe majority ownership in something. Write straight to the bottom.

While reading ______________________________

(book title)

____

(an ethnic-sounding last name)

____

(a very large number)

____

____

(an adjective that describes you first thing in the morning)

____

____

(*-ly* adverb describing how you walk)

____

____

(a game you enjoy)

____

(a foreign word)

____

(a hobby)

____

____

(name of a city you've never been to)

____

(a mode of transportation)

____

____

(a pet name)

TAKE THE NEXT STEP

If you tried Sbil Dam—One with a partner, try Sbil Dam—Two with a group. If you are leading the group, don't let anyone know they will be passing their paper to the left until after they fill in all the random words. The loud groan that everyone emits when they hear, "Pass your papers left," is very entertaining! When everyone is done writing, return the sheets to their original owners. The original owners decide if they want to share with the group.

Mother & Daughter

You are a mother shopping for clothes for the new school year with your teenage daughter. You don't approve of her choices. Start with: *I'm sorry, but it's too ...*

TAKE THE NEXT STEP

Make a list of life moments when your opinions differed from those of a parent. You will likely have a lot of good writing material in this list. Flesh out one of those moments today.

SNAPSHOTS 3

Write quick "word snapshots" for the following topics. Use your words as a camera lens, and capture colors, textures, and expressions. Use your own life story ... or make them up!

An embarrassing moment ...

A religious celebration ...

By a pool ...

In the snow ...

TAKE THE NEXT STEP

Capture a snapshot of the future by closing your eyes and picturing what you want. Do it now. Then take it one step further and envision the success that comes from writing: people listening to you read poetry, someone discovering your journal in one hundred years, an audience laughing at your romantic comedy, your article printed in a magazine or newspaper, your blog going viral, your writing helping someone heal, etc.

Start with: *I rarely get cross, but ...*

TAKE THE NEXT STEP

If you've ever gotten cross with a review of a book you've read, try writing a review yourself. Review a recent book, film, song, or article. Maybe you should submit it for publication.

SOUNDS touching

Write six sounds that are touching, such as a baby's coo or a cat's purr. Use them all in a story that begins as follows: *Lately I have been unable to tolerate ...*

TAKE THE NEXT STEP

Read aloud what you just wrote, listening to the sounds as if they were music. If a word, phrase, or sentence sounds "off," circle it. Now go back and edit or change the words you've circled. Continue to reread the piece out loud, making changes until it sounds touching and pleasant to your ear. That's a sign of good writing.

OVALTEEN

**Let the shapes aid your imagination as you write.
A starting phrase is provided for the first "football." Other directions follow.**

Just like a football, I ...

Use the last sentence from the piece you just completed to start a new writing in the second football.

TAKE THE NEXT STEP

Describe your current writing practice as if it were a colored shape. (Example: a soft twenty-six-sided brown blob with scattered neon-pink polka dots on the inside and outside.) What would you prefer it to look like? Get some markers, colored pencils, or crayons, and draw it.

SIMPLE SYMBOLS

Look at these forty simple symbols for about one minute. Close the book, and write (or draw if you prefer) on a blank piece of paper as many symbols as you can recall. Now reopen the book. You are going to use all the symbols you recalled (as well as any you may have mistakenly added to the mix) in a story.

Start with: *We called him Simple Simon ...*

TAKE THE NEXT STEP

What symbolizes writing success for you? Is it writing something every day? Finishing a story? Getting an agent? Writing the book you know is inside you? Finishing a memoir to give to your family? Getting your children's book into libraries? A textbook? Getting published? Self-publishing? A huge number of readers for your blog? Seeing your play performed? Licensing your screenplay? Walking the red carpet for your movie opening? A poetry chapbook? Greeting cards sold in stores? It's certainly different for everyone. Knowing what it is for you and being able to picture it means you are much more likely to see it become a reality and enjoy it while it is happening. Picture yours now.

adjacent adjectives

Use the adjacent adjectives on the page as you get to them. Start with: *We hugged ...*

red hot

smooth dark

cold wet

soft fuzzy

TAKE THE NEXT STEP

Comparing yourself to others is very detrimental to your creativity. Next time you find yourself doing this, generate a list of adjectives in your head. Every time you think of one that describes you and/or your writing practice, write it down. At the end of ten minutes, combine the adjectives to describe yourself. It will be different every time. Try it now.

setting sun

Set this story during an eclipse.
Start with: *The light was ...*

TAKE THE NEXT STEP

List six enlightening memories from your Octobers of yore. Use these to prompt further writings.

an **ear**ful

Finish these shorts. Starters are provided.

When the pencil got stuck in my ear ...

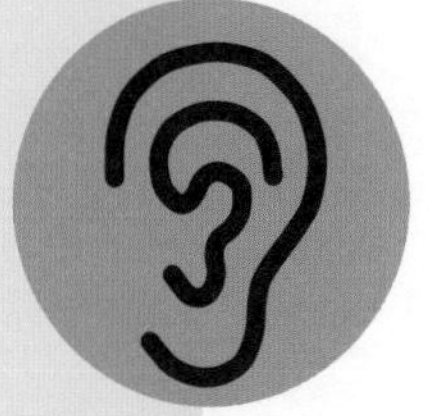

He had the biggest ears ...

She always kept her ear to the ground ...

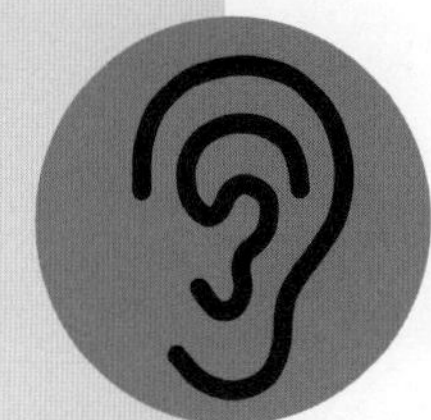

He could make his ears twitch and his ...

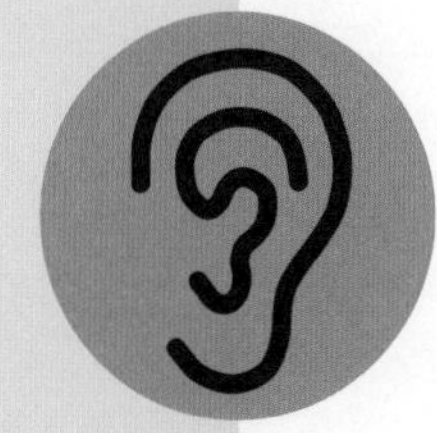

TAKE THE NEXT STEP

Here's a challenge for you: Write a paragraph without using the letters *E*, *A*, or *R*. Start with: *With two ...*

fair fare

Finish the story. Start with: *In his rearview mirror, the cab driver saw …*

TAKE THE NEXT STEP

Rather than beat ourselves up over where we are not or what we still have to learn, it's healthy to remind ourselves how much we know and how far we've come. Write two things you know now that you wish you had known when you started writing.

Take a minute (or longer if you choose) to complete each of these "if" scenarios.

IF MY WRITING WAS/WERE ...

Invisible, *I might not ...*

Illustrated, *others might ...*

Waterproof, *I would ...*

Edible, *I could ...*

Mobile, *I wouldn't ...*

Simpler, *it might ...*

Scented, *it would ...*

Wearable, *others could ...*

Life-size, *it could ...*

Airborne, *others would ...*

TAKE THE NEXT STEP

Here's another set of "ifs" for you:

If your writing were a package ...

... would you be the sender or the receiver?
... has it already been delivered?
... where is its ultimate destination?
... how is it being sent, or how was it sent?
... where will it (or did it) visit in transit?
... what is the weight of the package?
... what is the shape of the package?
... what's inside?

stepping-stones

In each of the three stepping-stones on this page, write about episodes from three separate stages in your life. All the episodes will revolve around the same word. Using *pink*, a color I don't really identify with, three memories came to mind: *pink cheeks in a camp photo, preteen pink lipstick, pink prom flowers.*

Pick a word to trigger writings about three different episodes in three different stages of your life.

Yellow

Pink

Sweat

Dust

Fence

Jump

Cereal

Light

Rain

Rock

TAKE THE NEXT STEP

Choose one item from your dream list of goals that you'd like to accomplish as a writer. On the top of a piece of paper, write down one thing you can do towards this goal in the next twenty-four hours. Below it, list one thing you can do towards this goal in the next week. Then write what you can do the week after that, and so on until you have listed all the major stepping-stones toward making this dream a reality. If looking at all the steps seems intimidating, don't worry; instead, fold the paper so that only the first stepping-stone on the list is showing. Once you accomplish this, open the paper to reveal the next stepping-stone, and so on. By taking it one stepping-stone at a time, you will stay in the present, make strides, and keep from worrying about what is to come.

factions of fractions

Use the fractions as you get to them. Start with: *If it appears as if I am thinking with a fraction of my brain ...*

$1/2$

$1/4$

$1/8$

$2/3$

$3/4$

$3/8$

TAKE THE NEXT STEP

Fill each of the sixteen boxes in the grid with a word taken from the writing you already did on this page. You'll end up with a poem that reads from left to right and from top to bottom.

Finish the story. Start with: *I met him in an online forum for ...*

TAKE THE NEXT STEP

The more people you meet and ask for help to accomplish your goals, the more likely you'll succeed. Make a list of people who can help you or who might know someone who can help. Ask one for assistance today.

Look around you, and notice all the *yellow* things. Write down the first six you see:

mellow yellow

Use all six. Start with: *One man's treasure is another man's ...*

TAKE THE NEXT STEP

Get some wrapping paper or newspaper (or tape together pieces of copy paper), and wrap this book. Tomorrow when you reach for it you'll be reminded just how much you treasure the gift of writing. Do this with other projects, too. It puts the way you approach and appreciate them in a whole new light. Start wrapping.

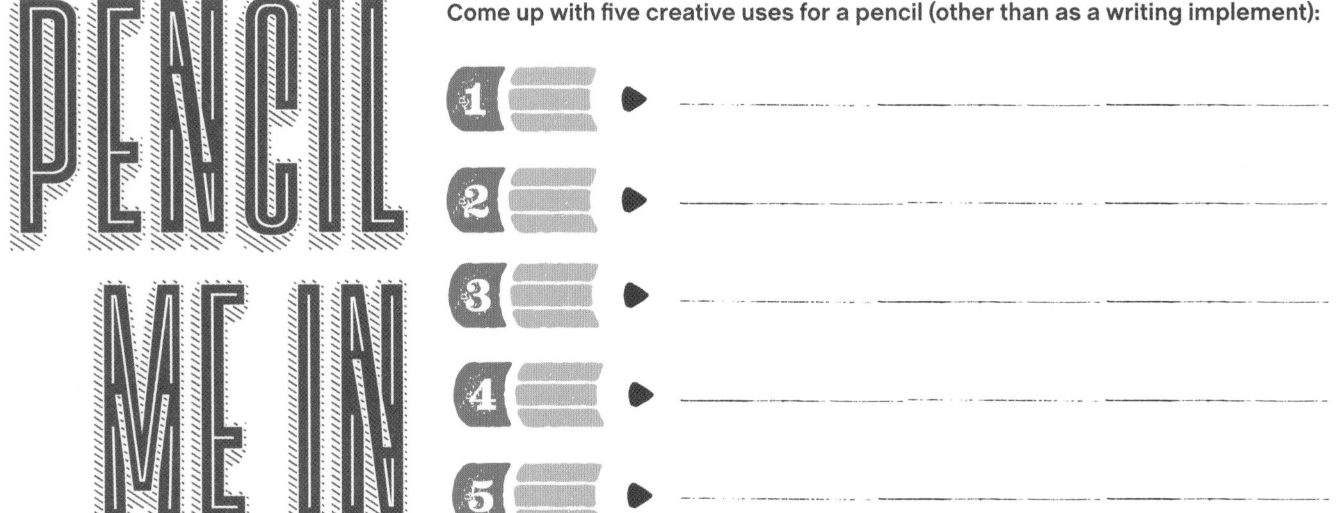

Incorporate these five "uses" in this piece. **START WITH:** *Whenever I am asked to ...*

TAKE THE NEXT STEP

Write a thank-you note to your pen, pencil, or keyboard. Butter it up. Don't feel silly—it's your partner. Where would Fred be without Ginger ... or Wilma?

THE DUMP

"Dumping" allows you to write whatever is floating in your mind that may or may not be full of good writing energy. Set a timer for ten minutes, and, starting with one of the words below, dump onto the page everything you feel, think, know, or want to know about this word. When something seems to push you to write more, go with it. Keep writing no matter how far from the original dump your topic may be. If this thread dries up before time runs out, return to your word and start over. You may be surprised at which items do and do not cause you to leave the original dump. Just go with it; the dump will always be there, waiting for you to return.

THUNDER
HOTDOG
UNIFORM
FLOATING
ROPE
SHOELACE
GARBAGE
LEMON
KITE

TAKE THE NEXT STEP

If you can't concentrate on your writing because too much of the day is swimming in your mind, try to identify each item that's taking up your mental time and dump them all onto an imaginary floor. Take an imaginary broom and sweep them into an imaginary satin bag. This bag of thoughts, worries, ideas, lists, memories, etc. will always be available to you, so let everything remain in the bag until after you finish your writing session ... or longer if you enjoy the light feeling of having dumped them.

lip service

Finish these shorts. Starters are provided.

She puckered her lips ...

Watching her apply lipstick ...

His lip curled whenever ...

His pouting lips ...

TAKE THE NEXT STEP

Make a long list of things that bring a smile to your lips, including three facets of writing.

Are you smiling now?

PHONE HOME

This info was taken from a suburban Philadelphia phone directory. Use your own local phone book—in print or online—to repeat the exercise!

TWO FIRST NAMES: Sandra, Arnold
TWO LAST NAMES: Chudnoff, Kramer
ONE RESTAURANT NAME: Lamb Tavern
ONE BEAUTY SALON NAME: WaveLength
ONE STREET NAME: Hampshire Drive

Now incorporate as many of the above items as possible into a piece. Start with: *The number was ...*

TAKE THE NEXT STEP

Does the phone ring if no one's around to hear it? Have you written something if you don't ever read it? Go back and read through some of the exercises you've done. Get a red pen, and circle the words and paragraphs that stand out. Pick up the phone, call your voice mail, and read some of these to yourself. Make them come alive.

P.T. BURN 'EM

Use all five of these words in this piece:

PAT POT PIT PET PUT

Start with: *There certainly is a sucker burned every minute. Take, for example, my ...*

TAKE THE NEXT STEP

When it comes to infomercials, I am a sucker. I want to buy everything. When the announcer says, "Wait, there's more," I get excited. Similar to performers doing an encore, what can you do to add extra oomph for your readers?

RAPID RECALL 2

Write the first thing that comes to mind, even if it's not at all true. Use the starters provided. Do all four at once. Don't stop to think—write fast!

I recall wincing ...

That's not at all how I recall what happened ...

I remember faces, but I never recall the names that go with them. For example ...

Recalling the past makes me want to ...

TAKE THE NEXT STEP

Whether you have a tendency to look back and recall life or to project forward in life, you can use it to your writing advantage. Look-backers can write memoir; look-aheaders can write science fiction. Based on this, brainstorm some ideas.

NOSE-Y

Write a smell you love here:

Now write a story incorporating this smell, starting with: *When I was ...*

Now think of a smell you hate and finish your story, incorporating this smell.

TAKE THE NEXT STEP
What does writing success smell like to you? Be very specific. Get something that reminds you of this smell, and inhale it often!

All My Life's a Circle • ONE

Circle the one word that most appeals to you:

helium circus rings balloon popcorn

Circle another word that appeals to you:

clown elephant laugh top tent

Circle yet another word that you find appealing:

tame tightrope acrobat master lion

Use your three chosen words in a story. Start with: *She shrugged her shoulders and said, "I don't know why ...*

TAKE THE NEXT STEP

Get a marker, crayon, or colored pencil, and draw circular, flowing swirls all over this page until you can no longer read what you just wrote. How did it feel when you were doing this? Was it easy for you, or hard?

Letting go is different for every person and for every piece. Remember: What you write in this book is practice.

Finish these shorts. Starters are provided.

Her hands were so delicate ...

He took my hand in his ...

The calluses on his hands ...

I have to hand it to you ...

TAKE THE NEXT STEP

Close your eyes, and picture the hands of someone near and dear to you. Hold on to the image until a story comes to you. Start writing that story.

DIAL A DIALOGUE

You are an actress who makes her living doing commercials. You are also the owner of a duplex. You live on the bottom floor and rent out the top floor to an undercover policeman. There's a little tension (actually, a *big* disagreement) between the two of you. Play it out through a dialogue over the phone.

YOU: *Every time you ...*

COP:

YOU:

COP:

YOU:

COP:

YOU:

COP:

YOU:

COP:

YOU:

COP:

... and since you're the writer, *you* get the last word!

YOU:

TAKE THE NEXT STEP

Every time you have an appointment, are you an early bird, right on time, late, or a no-show? Does your writing practice reflect this other life pattern? What can you do to achieve balance in both?

ONE FROM COLUMN A

Write down Column A first, continue down Column B, and finish in Column C. Start with: *The hot air balloon ...*

COLUMN A

COLUMN B

TAKE THE NEXT STEP

Writing progress is like a rising hot air balloon. Chart your course thus far with a time line, labeling where you started (wannabe), to where you are now (give it a description), to where you want to be in one year (describe it), and in five years (describe that, too).

COLUMN C

RE-STORE

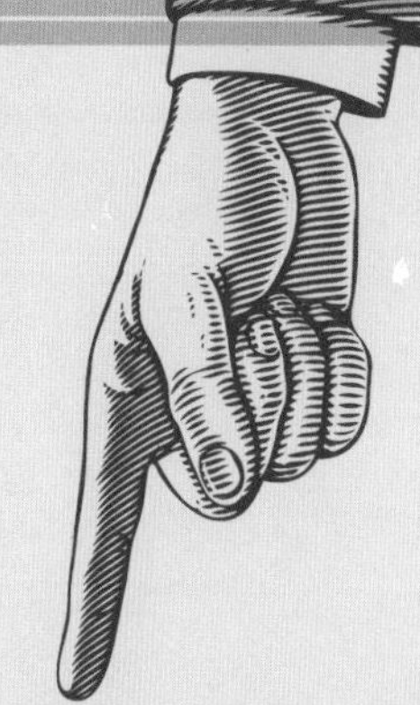

Take a mental visit to your favorite childhood store. Start with: *The funny thing about ...*

TAKE THE NEXT STEP

In my youth, my friends and I once pretended to case out the local five-and-ten store for a major break-in. What area of writing would you like to break in to? What's stopping you? Do something today that brings you closer to breaking in!

FLIPPER-TWO

Below are four backwards words. When you get to each word, flip it in your mind so it becomes a real word. Use that word in your story, before you get to the next word. (Don't read the words first—that spoils the fun!) Start with: *I remember laughing ...*

elcycib

ngis

ecaep

wollip

ezeeuqs

TAKE THE NEXT STEP

Do you link writing with pain or with pleasure? Why? What can you do to make it more pleasant?

FUN AND GAMES TWO

Use each word on the left side of the page as it appears. Start with: *Sometimes the most fun can be had ...*

monopoly

perfection

twister

outburst

cranium

risk

TAKE THE NEXT STEP

Gift giving and receiving both feel wonderful. Here's a chance to double your fun. What's the best inexpensive (or free) gift you can give your writer-self? Write steps on how you'll go about giving this gift to yourself.

RUN ON

Write one sentence consisting of twenty-six words where each word begins with consecutive letters of the alphabet. Start with the letter *R*. (Example: *Robert said that Ulysses vibrated William's xylophone yesterday zealously as Becky called David's eloquent father George Harrison Isaacson jokingly kidding losing many nice optimistic platitudes quickly.*) Hopefully yours will be better than mine!

R ______

S ______

T ______

U ______

V ______

W ______

X ______

Y ______

Z ______

A ______

B ______

C ______

D ______

E ______

F ______

G ______

H ______

I ______

J ______

K ______

L ______

M ______

N ______

O ______

P ______

Q ______

TAKE THE NEXT STEP

In twenty-six words or less, write a writing goal. Also in twenty-six words or less, write how you would feel one year from now if you attained this goal. Why deprive yourself of this feeling? Get started on that goal!

The Journalist and The Journaler

You are a twenty-one-year-old young woman from Germany about to marry an American journalist. The wedding is in two hours. You have been a devout journal keeper your whole life. Write your last entry as a single woman.

Start with: *The clock in this room ...*

TAKE THE NEXT STEP

Clocks tell more than time. Describe three clocks from your life.

1.
2.
3.

Give these descriptions a permanent home by dropping them directly into future writings.

Fall Leaves Me Wishing

Finish the story. *Every year in mid-October, we take a ride to the Pocono Mountains where we soak up the fall hues and visit my husband's colorful relatives. The trip always leaves me wishing ...*

TAKE THE NEXT STEP

Many creative people are colorful characters with beliefs that limit their ability to produce, such as believing they can only write if they have three fine-tip black felt pens. Do you have limiting beliefs? Sometimes they are subtle. List a way you can break through obstacles you put in your own way.

TWENTY QUESTIONS » TWO

Answer the twenty questions by circling one option. At the end of this exercise you'll have a character sketch.

1. Human or alien?
2. Big or little?
3. Hairy or no hair?
4. Devout or skeptical?
5. Mad or cheery?
6. Clairvoyant or oblivious?
7. Picky or undemanding?
8. Authentic or false?
9. Athletic or rotund?
10. Famous or infamous?
11. Indoorsy or outdoorsy?
12. Bold or wimpy?
13. Crayons or markers?
14. Travels by boat or by plane?
15. Flip phone or smartphone?
16. Board games or video games?
17. Reader or writer?
18. Pie or cake?
19. Boxers or briefs?
20. Paper or plastic?

You are this person or alien. Write from his, her, or its perspective. Start with: *I couldn't stop ...*

TAKE THE NEXT STEP

If your writer-self were a traffic sign, would you be a stop sign? A yield sign? A soft shoulder sign? How often do you break your own traffic rules? Do you need to choose another sign? Which one? Why?

All My Life's a Circle 2

CIRCLE TWO WORDS THAT APPEAL TO YOU:
mushroom
gemologist
moody
bungalow
debutante
taxi

CIRCLE TWO WORDS THAT APPEAL TO YOU:
carnivore
dill
miniature
hairy
telephone
temperature

CIRCLE TWO WORDS THAT APPEAL TO YOU:
rubber
squeeze
potion
aspirin
chalky
bananas

Use these six words in a story. Start with: *It was just after dark ...*

TAKE THE NEXT STEP

Turn out all the lights, and finish this statement while writing in total darkness: *I don't see why ...*

August Augmentation

You are a public school teacher. You love your job, but you *really* love your summer vacation. As the warmth of August nears to an end, you wish and pray for it to somehow magically extend ... and *it does!* Write the story. Start with: *Sometimes dreams ...*

TAKE THE NEXT STEP

List six dreams or realities from the Augusts of your life. Use these to prompt further writings.

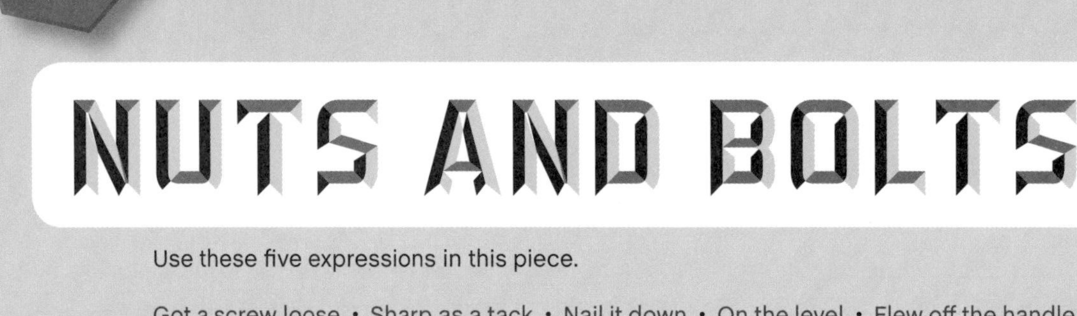

NUTS AND BOLTS

Use these five expressions in this piece.

Got a screw loose • Sharp as a tack • Nail it down • On the level • Flew off the handle

Start with: *It hit me like a ton of bricks ...*

TAKE THE NEXT STEP

Get down to the nuts and bolts of writing—nailing down quotation marks. Quotation marks are used to:

- represent text as speech.
- indicate material excerpted from another writer.
- indicate titles of poems, essays, and short stories.

Remember these rules for quotation marks:

- Periods and commas go inside the closing quotation mark.
- Colons, semicolons, dashes, question marks, and exclamation points go outside unless they're part of the quotation.

MORE OR *less*

If you've been consistently writing for at least ten minutes or for some other steady time frame or page count, it's time to shake things up a bit. For this exercise, intentionally write for more or less time (or pages) than usual. For instance, if you've been writing for ten minutes, up the ante to twenty; if you're pressed for time, cut it down to five.

On the *less* side, it's important to remind yourself you can fit in a good writing session in a very short period of time. When you don't have ten minutes, that doesn't mean you skip the day; it means you write for three or five minutes to keep up your momentum. On the *more* side, pushing yourself to keep the pen moving for a longer time gives you the opportunity to write deeper and see how that feels. If you like the results, schedule some longer writing sessions when you can.

Choose a "more or less" writing topic.

1. A time when you got less than you hoped or bargained for.
2. A time when you gave more than you thought you should have.
3. A time when you gave less than was expected.
4. A time when you prepared less than you should have.
5. A time when you took more than you should have.

TAKE THE NEXT STEP

In the business of writing, it helps to be an optimist who can see *more* when the initial tendency is to see *less*. For example:

1. A rejection is seen as one step closer to an acceptance.
2. Cutting out huge chunks of material that you love gives you a wealth of bonus information to post on your website or blog.

Practice finding the silver lining (where the more lives), and you will be a happier writer.

NOT GUILTY

Finish the story. Start with: *It was a time of innocence ...*

TAKE THE NEXT STEP

I confess: I don't exercise. Whenever I walk past any exercise equipment, I feel guilty. What habit in your writing practice makes you guilty? Can you eliminate it?

EN-TITLE-MENT

Write the first titles that come to mind.

Titles of two books:

Titles of two songs:

Titles of two magazines:

Choose one of these as the title of your story, and then use the other five in the content of what you write. They don't have to be used as titles at all. For example, if you chose the song "Leaving on a Jet Plane," you could use it as a phrase instead.

Your story title:

TAKE THE NEXT STEP

Among other things, a title should be concise, catchy, positive, and memorable.

Go back to an exercise of your choice and generate a list of titles for it.

In one week come back and see which title fits best!

TIME TRAVELER

Here's an opportunity to travel back in time and write short, unrelated paragraphs about four real-life events (or partially real-life events) from your past.

Pick a series of four topics about which you will write four unrelated, short paragraphs.

1. a birthday, corn, your thumb, a dog
2. toes, a cake, a compass, swimming
3. vanilla, a scar, wanting something, a prize
4. a flashlight, potatoes, a mistake, a neighbor
5. your knee, onions, missing out, stars
6. an ocean, grapes, a big purchase, sneezing
7. chewing gum, waiting, a wish, your hair
8. a female relative, cookies, a bicycle, coffee
9. a competition, a towel, a male relative, cereal
10. your stomach, tomatoes, a bathing suit, getting hurt

For all four paragraphs, start with this phrase:
I wasn't ...

TAKE THE NEXT STEP

If you're tracking your writing progress by time spent writing but find you're procrastinating a lot ... STOP. Start tracking your procrastination time instead. Getting a grip on when you procrastinate (in terms of the time of day or the phase of your creative process) is valuable information. Once you determine a pattern, you will be able to channel your time and energy in such a way that stops contributing to the procrastination and allows you to do more writing.

A N T I C I P A T I O N

Write a story about something that is just about to happen. Start with: *I was about to burst ...*

TAKE THE NEXT STEP

Let go of anticipation. As in sports like tennis and baseball, where you need to keep your eye on the ball, keep your pen on the paper. Don't lift it up. Should you get stuck, write the last word over and over until something comes. Do that now. Now, now, now.

F1ST RST F1ST RST'S

Here's a fun way to generate first phrases for writing exercises. Use the letters of your first name as the first letters of each of the first words in the first sentence of your story. For example, my name (*Bonnie*) might generate the phrase: *Because Olivia Never Needed It, Everyone ...*

Generate five first phrases using the letters in your name here:

FIRST PHRASE 1: __________

FIRST PHRASE 2: __________

FIRST PHRASE 3: __________

FIRST PHRASE 4: __________

FIRST PHRASE 5: __________

Pick your favorite **FIRST PHRASE** and write it on the line below. Then fill the page with the rest of the story.

TAKE THE NEXT STEP

Write the names of two people in the writing or publishing world with whom you would like to make contact:

1. __________

2. __________

Write the first step in the process of making this wish come true:

1. __________

When you complete step 1, should you require future steps, come back and write step 2 here:

2. __________

Often a simple search on Twitter, LinkedIn, or Facebook will get you in touch with some of your idols. And many *will* indeed write back.

START-UP

When it comes to starting phrases, you can never have too many in your writing tool kit. Start at the top of this list, and finish each sentence right now. If a sentence you create triggers your fancy, grab a sheet of paper and run with it, writing until you feel like stopping. Come back to this list another day and either start where you left off or pick one of the sentences you already created and start writing.

TAKE THE NEXT STEP

The key to a good start-up is a solid business plan. Writing practice is no different; you also need a plan. What is your plan for writing today? How about tomorrow? The rest of the week? Next week? The week after that? The next month? The rest of the year? Start up a plan right now for the next week, and try to stick with it. If it works, make a plan for an entire month.

After the storm ...

As if in slow motion, I watched the ...

As soon as I stepped on the ...

At the fork in the road ...

At the Santa training school ...

At the time it didn't seem risky ...

Basking in the ...

Behind the reflective sunglasses ...

Being low man on the totem pole ...

Blushing red as a beet, Erin ...

Born into poverty ...

Bright flashes of light sped ...

Carl was a watchman at ...

Chewing on her fingernails ...

Clandestinely in my basement, I printed ...

Dressed in a turtle costume ...

Drifting off into ...

Even the detectives were ...

Every afternoon while her baby slept, she ...

Floating in the mouth of the river ...

Free as a kite, I ...

From the sidelines ...

Greta sent in the sweepstakes entry form ...

Had she not mentioned ...

Hanging on the ...

He caught the trolley ...

He spit out ...

Her fate was decided the moment ...

Her lower lip quivered ...

THANKS, BUT NO TANKS

List three things from the past 365 days for which you are thankful.

1. ______________________________

2. ______________________________

3. ______________________________

Use all three items in a story in which you are a container-delivery person. Start with: *The aquarium workers were on strike, and I couldn't just leave the tank of sharks in the parking lot, so I ...*

TAKE THE NEXT STEP

Think about your writer-self over the last twenty-four hours. Did you accomplish anything? Why or why not? Were you the best writer you could be? Why or why not? Did you thank your writer-self? How? Let your answers guide the next twenty-four hours.

On the Road Again

Finish the story. Start with: *Moving ...*

TAKE THE NEXT STEP

The energy of others can move us forward. If you bring your writing goals to fruition, who else will benefit? How? Use their energy to move your writing not only forward but also up to the next level.

TWEET TWEET

Time to try your hand at some shorthand ... in the form of a tweet, which has a maximum of 140 characters, including spaces and punctuation. You are a ninety-year-old who is reluctantly (at the urging of a great-granddaughter) tweeting for the very first time. Use the starting characters in the preset 140-character areas. It would be sweet if these three tweets told a whole story.

M Y _ G R

F O R G

W H

TAKE THE NEXT STEP

Think twice before hitting the send button once. (Sometimes it only takes forty-eight characters to make a point.)

IDIOMS DELIGHT FOUR

Start with the idiom *He'll never set the world on fire.*

Use the idiomatic expression *Fish or cut bait* in your conclusion.

TAKE THE NEXT STEP

If the dictionary police asked you to help define a new word, what definition would you supply for *kwit*? Do you realize you just redefined the word *quit*? Remember: Words are only as powerful as you make them.

Snapshots Four

Write quick "word snapshots" for these life events. Try to capture colors, textures, and expressions as if your words were a camera. Use your own life story ... or make them up!

Learning to ride a bicycle:

In a costume:

A new car:

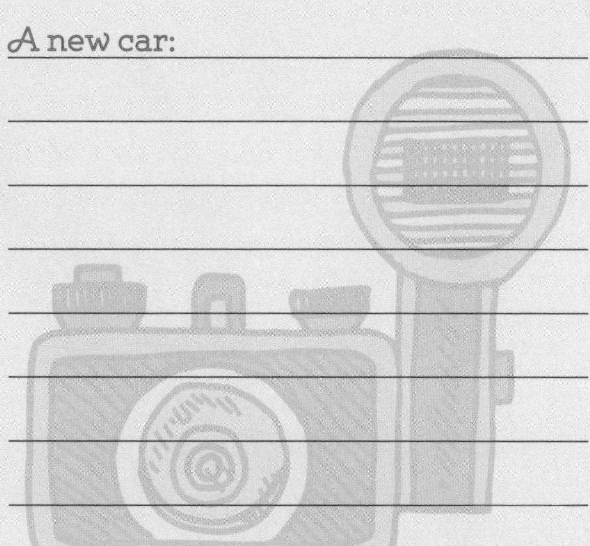

A contagious smile:

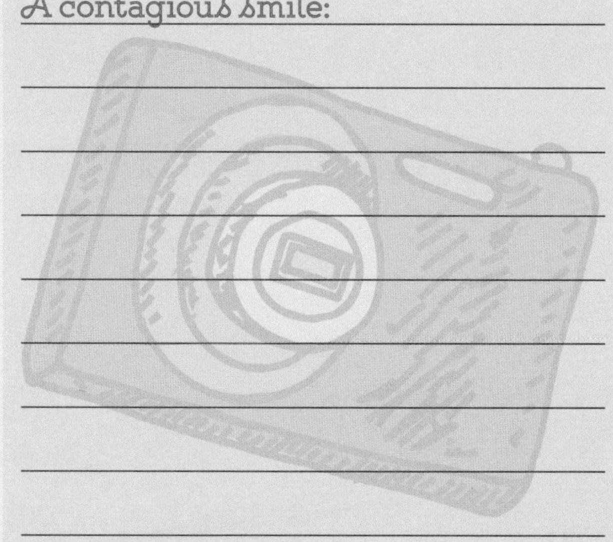

TAKE THE NEXT STEP

Picture your writing-self as a house. What ideas do you keep in each of these rooms? Is it time to move some of them?

- powder room
- master bedroom
- attic
- spare bedroom

OPERATION *Opera*

Finish this sentence, and use it in your story.

Like watching an opera, it reminded me that ... ______________________________

____

Start with: *The covert operation was ...*

TAKE THE NEXT STEP

If your muse were to take you out on a date, where do you think he or she would take you? The opera? A monster truck rally? An orchard? Fishing? An amusement park? The moon? Why?

QUICK XYLOPHONES JUMP ZEALOUSLY

Here's a combined word game and writing challenge that uses the four letters with the highest point values from a classic word game. The letters are Q (ten points), *Z* (ten points), *X* (eight points), and *J* (eight points).

Your goals are to:

1. Fill the twenty lines on this page using the starter provided by writing a cohesive and (hopefully) logical story. It's okay if your story does not draw to a close at the end of line 20.
2. Make sure each of the twenty lines contains at least one word with either a Q or a *Z* in it. They can start or end the word, or fall in the middle.
3. If you can't come up with a Q or *Z* word for a line, then do the next best thing: Use a word with either a *J* or an *X* on these lines. Once again, the *J* or *X* can be at the start, end, or middle of the word.

When you are done writing, count up your score as follows:

1. For every line that does *not* have a word with at least one Q, *Z*, *J*, or *X*, subtract ten points.
2. For every line with at least one word containing a Q or a *Z*, add ten points for the entire line.
3. For every line without a Q or *Z* but with at least one word containing a *J* or an *X*, add eight points for the entire line.

A perfect score (twenty lines multiplied by ten points per line) is 200, where every line has at least one word that contains either a Q or a *Z*.

Start with: *Whenever there's a full moon ...*

1. ______
2. ______
3. ______
4. ______
5. ______
6. ______
7. ______
8. ______
9. ______
10. ______
11. ______
12. ______
13. ______
14. ______
15. ______
16. ______
17. ______
18. ______
19. ______
20. ______

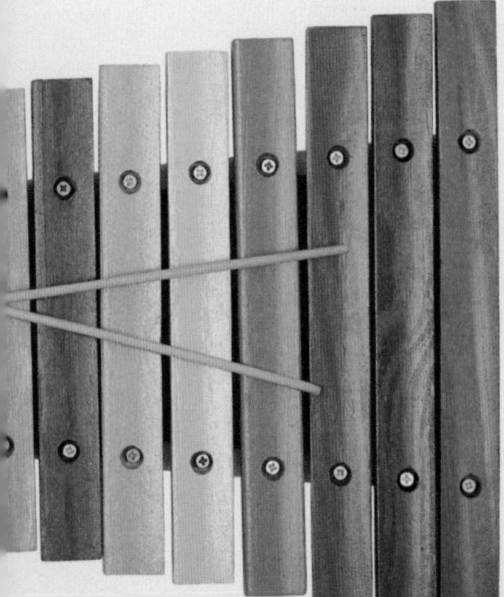

TAKE THE NEXT STEP

If you were to compare your writing practice or discipline to the sound of a musical instrument, would it be a xylophone, drums, saxophone, violin, cymbals, or some other instrument? If you think something else would sound better, alter your writing practice accordingly.

OPEN DOOR POLICY

"WHEN ONE DOOR CLOSES ANOTHER DOOR OPENS; BUT WE SO OFTEN LOOK SO LONG AND SO REGRETFULLY UPON THE CLOSED DOOR, THAT WE DO NOT SEE THE ONES WHICH OPEN FOR US." —Alexander Graham Bell

Like the above quote from Bell, I hope you choose to see the last exercise of this book not as an ending but as a chance for yet another new beginning where you continue to grow with your writing. Today's exercise will keep you from focusing on the door that is closing and, instead, dwell on the door that is opening.

Choose from one of these door-related starters:

1. *She lived in a building with a doorman ...*
2. *I ended the conversation by saying that I'd leave the door open ...*
3. *Whenever he turned a doorknob, he always slid his sleeve over his hand so ...*
4. *Of all the places I've lived, the one door that stands out the most is ...*
5. *Had I known there was a trapdoor and that one of us would fall through it ...*

Remember: This book is not really over, because many of the exercises can be done multiple times. All you have to do is flip through the book until you find this symbol and you are good to go.

TAKE THE NEXT STEP

Cut out a badge-shaped piece of paper. Write your full name on the top, and then, underneath it, write a maximum of fifteen words that are nice, kind, and complimentary about yourself as a writer. Tape it to the cover of this book the same way you would affix a scouting badge to a sash. You have definitely earned it! Congrats!

CREDITS

DESIGNERS

CLAUDEAN WHEELER: 1–19, 21–23, 26, 27, 29

ZACH NICOLAS: 20, 24, 25, 28, 30, 215–221, 226–229, 290–302, 304–306, 369, 371, 372, 374, 377, 378

ALEXIS BROWN: 31–60, 120, 122, 318, 337

GEOFF RAKER: 61–86

BAMBI EITEL: 87–112

ELYSE SCHWANKE: 113–119, 121, 123–138

BRIANNA SCHARSTEIN: 139–164

LAURA KAGEMANN: 165–177, 190–214

BRIAN ROETH: 178–189, 240-264

JENNIFER HOFFMAN: 222–225, 230–239

DAN PESSELL: 265–289

CLARE FINNEY: 303, 307–314

RONSON SLAGLE: 315–317, 319–336, 338, 339

JULIE BARNETT: 340–364

ADAM LADD: 365–368, 370, 373, 375, 376, 379–389

IMAGE CREDITS

1 Fotolia.com/Rachel Arnott; **2** Fotolia.com/Andrey Kuzman; **3** Fotolia.com/muchmania; **4** Fotolia.com/Galina Pankratova; **6** Fotolia.com/grgroup; **11** Fotolia.com/mangpor2004; **12** Fotolia.com/incomible; **13** Fotolia.com/siraphol; **14** Fotolia.com/Okea; **16** Fotolia.com/pywork; **17** Fotolia.com/moypapaboris; **18** Fotolia.com/Thanks For Purchase; **21** Fotolia.com/exopixel; **22** Fotolia.com/Omar Kulos; **23** Fotolia.com/Sergey Drozdov; **24** Shutterstock.com/Marish; **25** Zach Nicholas; **26** Fotolia.com/erika8213; **27** Fotolia.com/BillionPhotos.com; **29** Fotolia.com/vetalgard; **30** Zach Nicholas; **31** Shutterstock.com/Ameu; **32** Fotolia.com/CurvaBezier; **33** Shutterstock.com/Micra; **34** Shutterstock.com/vvvisual; **35** Shutterstock.com/Complot; **36** Shutterstock.com/snapgalleria; **37** Shutterstock.com/smilewithjul; **38** Shutterstock.com/Doremi; **39** Shutterstock.com/kmlmtz66; **41** Shutterstock.com/MikeMcDonald; **42** Shutterstock.com/g/ martynmarin; **43** Shutterstock.com/Doremi; **44** Shutterstock.com/g/karnoff; **45** Shutterstock.com/mymayday; **46** Shutterstock.com/Doremi; 47 Shutterstock.com/mhatzapa; **48** Fotolia.com/CurvaBezier; **49** Shutterstock.com/jorgenmcleman; **50** Shutterstock.com/lavitrei; **51** Shutterstock.com/IvanNikulin; **52** Shutterstock.com/Seita; **53** Fotolia.com/stocksolutions; **54** Shutterstock.com/IakovKalinin; **55** Shutterstock.com/kotoffei; **56** Shutterstock.com/openeyed; **57** Shutterstock.com/Complot; **58** Shutterstock.com/Happy_Inside; **59** Shutterstock.com/Dooder; **60** Shutterstock.com/lyeyee; **61** Fotolia.com/greatandlittle; **62** Fotolia.com/Style-o-Mat; **63** Fotolia.com/CurvaBezier; **64** Fotolia.com/Becker, Fotolia.com/windu; **65** Fotolia.com/sergio34; **66** Fotolia.com/natbasil; **67** Fotolia.com/sukporn; **68** Fotolia.com/BillionPhotos.com; **69** Fotolia.com/WildOrchid; **70** Fotolia.com/fiore26; **71** Fotolia.com/luigi giordano; **72** Fotolia.com/Capeman29; **73** Fotolia.com/sveta; **74** Fotolia.com/Danomyte; **75** Fotolia.com/okalinichenko; **76** Fotolia.com/Maksim Pasko; **77** Fotolia.com/GstudioGroup; **78** Fotolia.com/karandaev; **79** Fotolia.com/445017; **80** Fotolia.com/olly; **81** Fotolia.com/Oculo; **82** Fotolia.com/Cindy Xiao, Fotolia.com/stokkete, Fotolia.com/nikolarakic; **83** Fotolia.com/stuart, Fotolia.com/AlexanderNovikov, **84** Fotolia.com/chab3; **85** Fotolia.com/Dessie; **86** Fotolia.com/AfricaStudio; **87** Fotolia.com/Anna Kucherova; **88** Fotolia.com/~ Bitter ~; **89** Fotolia.com/incomible; **90** Fotolia.com/ufotopixl10; **91** Fotolia.com/melindula; **92** Fotolia.com/AbsentAnna; **93** Fotolia.com/Login; **94** Fotolia.com/mangpor2004; **95** Fotolia.com/Real Illusion; **96** Fotolia.com/avian; **98** Fotolia.com/eobrazy_pl; **99** Fotolia.com/Dooder; **100** Fotolia.com/kaktus2536; **101** Fotolia.com/Lonely; **102** Fotolia.com/Dejan Jovanovic, Fotolia.com/piai; **103** Fotolia.com/baluchis; **104** Fotolia.com/boomingpie; **105** Fotolia.com/baluchis; **106** Fotolia.com/slybrowney; **107** Fotolia.com/Transfuchsian; **108** Fotolia.com/Ildogesto; **109** Fotolia.com/PrettyVectors; **110** Fotolia.com/beachboyx10; **111** Fotolia.com/depiano; **112** Fotolia.com/olgash_i; **113** Fotolia.com/Rawpixel; **114** Elyse Schwanke; **115** Elyse Schwanke; **116** Fotolia.com/Pakhnyushchyy; **117** Elyse Schwanke; **118** Elyse Schwanke; **119** Fotolia.com/oly5, Elyse Schwanke; **120** Shutterstock.com/KakigoriStudio; **121** Fotolia.com/magnia; **122** Shutterstock.com/Ezepov Dmitry; **123** Elyse Schwanke; **124** Fotolia.com/Iveta Angelova; **125** Elyse Schwanke; **126** Fotolia.com/Igor Serazetdinov, Elyse Schwanke; **127** Fotolia.com/ngocdai86; **129** Elyse Schwanke; **130** Elyse Schwanke; **131** Fotolia.com/Petr Vaclavek, Fotolia.com/pixelrobot, Fotolia.com/Georgios Kollidas; **132** Fotolia.com/sararoom, Fotolia.com/Ekaterina

Molodtsova, Elyse Schwanke; **133** Fotolia.com/dimakp, Elyse Schwanke; **135** Fotolia.com/tackgalichstudio; **136** Fotolia.com/natbasil, Elyse Schwanke; **137** Elyse Schwanke; **138** Fotolia.com/rtguest, Elyse Schwanke; **139** Fotolia.com/KirstyPargeter; **140** Fotolia.com/eatcute; **141** Fotolia.com/merydolla; **142** Fotolia.com/Denchik; **143** Brianna Scharstein; **144** Fotolia.com/karandaev; **145** Fotolia.com/vatrushka; **146** Brianna Scharstein; **147** Fotolia.com/reich; **148** Fotolia.com/riedja, Fotolia.com/mesamong, Fotolia.com/swillklitch; **150** Fotolia.com/thirteenfifty; **151** Fotolia.com/Africa Studio, Fotolia.com/AlenKadr; **153** Fotolia.com/Mikrobiuz; **154** Fotolia.com/blueringmedia; **155** Fotolia.com/Igor; **157** Fotolia.com/Rorius; **158** Fotolia.com/fireflamenco; **159** Fotolia.com/Lonely; **160** Fotolia.com/karandaev; **161** Fotolia.com/Anna-Mari West, Fotolia.com/rtguest; **162** Fotolia.com/Orlando Florin Rosu; **163** Fotolia.com/RetroClipArt, Fotolia.com/ferumov; **164** Fotolia.com/Galyna Andrushko; **165** Fotolia.com/Frog 974; **166** Fotolia.com/palau83; **167** Fotolia.com/hofred; **168** Fotolia.com/nuttapol, Fotolia.com/iuneWind; **169** Fotolia.com/macrovector; **170** Fotolia.com/rashadashurov; **171** Fotolia.com/valeo5, Fotolia.com/eatcute; **172** Fotolia.com/lightgirl; **174** Fotolia.com/scol22; **176** Laura Kagemann; **177** Fotolia.com/rashadashurov; **178** Fotolia.com/Eric Isselée, Fotolia.com/Carolyn Franks, Fotolia.com/anankkml, Fotolia.com/viperagp, Fotolia.com/worldofvector; **179** Fotolia.com/mizar_21984; **180** Fotolia.com/chones; **181** Fotolia.com/worldofvector; **182** Fotolia.com/nortivision; **183** Fotolia.com/katrinaelena; **184** Fotolia.com/Sura Nualpradid; **185** Fotolia.com/picsfive, Fotolia.com/pressmaster; **186** Fotolia.com/mimacz, Fotolia.com/vladvm50, Fotolia.com/Gstudio Group, Fotolia.com/Dimitar Marinov, Fotolia.com/logistock, Fotolia.com/teracreonte, Fotolia.com/oxyggen, Fotolia.com/koolander, Fotolia.com/RA Studio; **187** Fotolia.com/Ekler; **188** Fotolia.com/picsfive; **189** Fotolia.com/bramgino; **190** Fotolia.com/Danussa; **191** Fotolia.com/cirodelia; **192** Laura Kagemann; **193** Fotolia.com/nokastudio; **194** Fotolia.com/cunico; **195** Fotolia.com/hypnocreative; **196** Fotolia.com/click_and_photo; **199** Fotolia.com/Bartlomiej Zyczynski; **200** Fotolia.com/kittitee550; **201** Fotolia.com/Neo Edmund; **202** Fotolia.com/podshibykin; **203** Fotolia.com/okalinichenko; **205** Fotolia.com/cirodelia; **206** Fotolia.com/Lonely; **207** Fotolia.com/jodo19; **208** Fotolia.com/emuemu; **209** Fotolia.com/archideaphoto; **210** Laura Kagemann; **211** Fotolia.com/adimas; **212** Laura Kagemann; **213** Fotolia.com/Iveta Angelova; **217** Fotolia.com/Wissanu99; **218** Fotolia.com/olliethedesigner; **219** Fotolia.com/Wissanu99; **222** Fotolia.com/2xSamara.com, Fotolia.com/serkucher; **223** Fotolia.com/kyoko; **225** Fotolia.com/GiuseppePorzani; **226** Fotolia.com/archideaphoto; **228** Fotolia.com/Andrii Pokaz; **229** Fotolia.com/9comeback; **230** Fotolia.com/Casther; **231** Fotolia.com/magann; **232** Fotolia.com/kmit; **233** Fotolia.com/Irochka; **234** Fotolia.com/frozenmost; **235** Fotolia.com/Alexander Zelnitskiy; **236** Fotolia.com/Feng Yu; **237** Fotolia.com/dwph, Fotolia.com/Neptune; **238** Fotolia.com/eyeretina; **239** Fotolia.com/mysontuna; **240** Fotolia.com/Daniel Heywood; **241** Fotolia.com/fotomatrix; **242** Fotolia.com/zhelunovych; **243** Fotolia.com/HieroGraphic; **244** Fotolia.com/Rada Covalenco; **245** Fotolia.com/najtli; **246** Fotolia.com/sunny_lion; **247** Fotolia.com/rudall30; **248** Fotolia.com/aeroking; **249** Fotolia.com/LeonART, Fotolia.com/mhatzapa; **250** Fotolia.com/RetroClipArt; **251** Fotolia.com/picsfive; **252** Fotolia.com/Sveta; **253** Fotolia.com/Anna Frajtova; **254** Fotolia.com/romvo; **255** Fotolia.com/Seamartini Graphics; **256** Fotolia.com/Adrian Niederhäuser; **257** Fotolia.com/Nik_Merkulov; **258** Fotolia.com/noscovaolga; **259** Fotolia.com/marforrstock; **260** Fotolia.com/th3fisa; **261** Fotolia.com/Fotographix; **262** Fotolia.com/chones; **263** Fotolia.com/Ekaterina Garyuk; **264** Fotolia.com/shadowalice; **265** Fotolia.com/Sylwia Nowik; **266** Fotolia.com/Maksim Shebeko, Fotolia.com/loreanto; **267** Fotolia.com/goodween123; **268** Fotolia.com/wayne_0216, Fotolia.com/jineshgopikklm, Fotolia.com/Ljupco Smokovski; **269** Fotolia.com/jonnysek; **271** Fotolia.com/photosvac; **272** Fotolia.com/fotoatelie; **273** Fotolia.com/elophotos; **274** Fotolia.com/Gianfranco Bella; **275** Fotolia.com/eugenesergeev; **276** Fotolia.com/Arsgera; **277** Dan Pessell; **278** Fotolia.com/ra2 studio, Fotolia.com/Virynja; **279** Fotolia.com/Photobank; **280** Fotolia.com/tomo; **281** Fotolia.com/Irochka; **282** Fotolia.com/Ljupco Smokovski; **283** Fotolia.com/Dmytro Sukharevskyy; **284** Fotolia.com/cirodelia; **285** Fotolia.com/sutichak; **286** Dan Pessell; **287** Fotolia.com/zsooofija; **288** Fotolia.com/jonbilous; **289** Fotolia.com/tinadefortunata; **290** Zach Nicholas; **291** Fotolia.com/Garry Images; **292** Zach Nicholas; **293** Zach Nicholas; **294** Zach Nicholas; **295** Fotolia.com/Aleksandra Novakovic, Zach Nicholas; **296** Zach Nicholas; **297** Zach Nicholas; **298** Fotolia.com/girafchik; **299** Zach Nicholas; **300** Fotolia.com/lestyan; **301** Zach Nicholas; **302** Zach Nicholas; **303** Fotolia.com/Jorge Alejandro; **304** Zach Nicholas; **305** Zach Nicholas; **306** Fotolia.com/eatcute; **307** Fotolia.com/rtguest, Fotolia.com/patrimonio designs; **308** Fotolia.com/mattasbestos, Fotolia.com/liravega.ai; **309** Fotolia.com/jesadaphorn; **310** Fotolia.com/dule964, Fotolia.com/Uros Petrovic; **311** Fotolia.com/headcircle, Fotolia.com/eat cute; **312** Fotolia.com/00798; **313** Fotolia.com/photoestelar 3; **314** Fotolia.com/Rada Covalenco; **315** Ronson Slagle; **316** Fotolia.com/Giorgio Clementi; **317** Ronson Slagle; **318** Shutterstock.com/veron_ice; **319** Ronson Slagle; **320** Ronson Slagle; **322** Ronson Slagle; **324** Fotolia.com/Sebastian Kaulitzki; **325** Fotolia.com/bannosuke; **326** Fotolia.com/Julia Tim; **327** Fotolia.com/Meliha Gojak; **329** Fotolia.com/aaabbc; **331** Ronson Slagle; **334** Ronson Slagle; **339** Fotolia.com/Ludmila Baryshnikova; **340** Fotolia.com/Andrey Kuzmin; **342** Fotolia.com/evgenyi; **343** Fotolia.com/aopsan; **344** Fotolia.com/rashadashurov; **346** Fotolia.com/MassimoSaivezzo; **347** Fotolia.com/ilqarsm; **348** Fotolia.com/ra3rn.tif, Fotolia.com/rashadashurov; **350** Fotolia.com/MG1408, Fotolia.com/teerawat_camt, Fotolia.com/Oksana; **355** Fotolia.com/calmacanul; **357** Fotolia.com/brat82; **358** Fotolia.com/binik; **360** Fotolia.com/Fly_dragonfly; **361** Fotolia.com/Kudryashka; **363** Fotolia.com/Masson; **364** Fotolia.com/~Bitter~; **365** Fotolia.com/lestyan; **366** Fotolia.com/studiostoks; **367** Fotolia.com/denis_pc; **370** Fotolia.com/Lonely; **373** Fotolia.com/sundarananda; **376** Fotolia.com/BillionPhotos.com; **382** Fotolia.com/molowpoly; **383** Fotolia.com/karandaev; **386** Fotolia.com/macrovector; **387** Fotolia.com/olegdudko; **388** Fotolia.com/Constantinos; 389 Fotolia.com/archideaphoto

ALSO FROM BONNIE NEUBAUER...

STORY SPINNER

Story Spinner is a handheld creative writing wheel that generates millions of writing exercises so you never have to face a blank page. It's a low-tech item that produces high-caliber results, time after time after time.

Story Spinner is perfect for:

- **TEACHERS:** It's an instant creative writing lesson plan.
- **WRITERS:** Never be blocked again.
- **PARENTS:** Encourage your kids' creativity in a fun way.
- **STUDENTS:** Finally, help with creative writing assignments.
- **IMPROV ACTORS AND STORYTELLERS:** Spin the wheels as you go.
- **GIFTS:** For that creative person in your life ... or yourself!

Here's an example of a prompt generated by spinning the three Story Spinner wheels:

1. The purple wheel provides a phrase to start your story. Yours is "The best hiding place ..."
2. The black wheel gives you a setting to locate your story. Yours is "during a war"
3. The red wheel generates words you must include in your story. Yours are "roller coaster, pickle, disguise"

Now set a timer for ten minutes, or set a goal to write one entire page, using all the items from the wheels. You'll be amazed at the results.

To spin stories right away, an online Story Spinner awaits you at www.BonnieNeubauer.com. Return as often as you like; there are millions of writing exercises that can be generated for your writing pleasure.

To buy your very own handheld, portable Story Spinner that you can use even if there's no Wi-Fi available, please PayPal $10.99 per Spinner (this price includes shipping in the U.S.) to account neubon@gmail.com. Or send a check or money order to Bonnie Neubauer, P.O. Box 810, Ardmore, PA 19083. For international purchases or bulk orders for schools, writing groups, or resale, please call 610-446-7441 or send an e-mail to neubon@gmail.com.

ALSO FROM WRITER'S DIGEST BOOKS

THE WRITER'S IDEA THESAURUS
by Fred White
This resource is more than just a loose collection of writing prompts—it's a valuable, organized list of 2,000 ideas. With sections on subject, genre, situation, and more, you can easily battle writer's block and land on the perfect story idea.

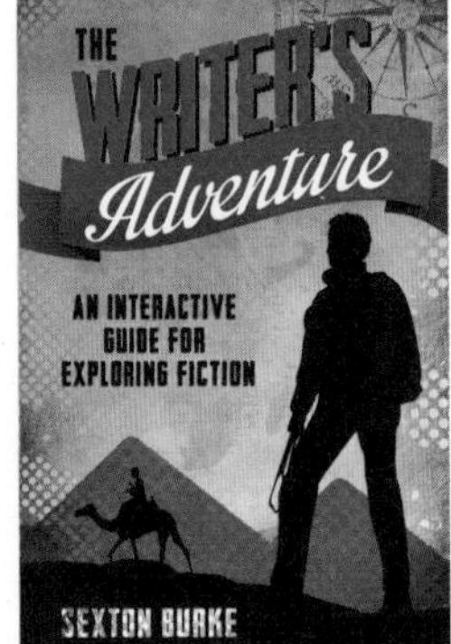

THE WRITER'S ADVENTURE
by Sexton Burke
This book provides writers, journalers, and creatives with a medium for experimenting with creative writing and poetry. There are no rules here—only creative prompts and plenty of room for writing, sketching, diagramming, and planning stories, characters, and more.